HORSE COP

OTHER BOOKS BY ROBERT J. ADAMS

* * *

THE STUMP FARM

BEYOND THE STUMP FARM

HORSE COP

ROBERT J. ADAMS

MEGAMY

THE PUBLISHER:
Megamy Publishing Ltd.
P. O. Box 3507
Spruce Grove, Alberta, Canada T7X 3A7
E-Mail megamy@compusmart.ab.ca

Canadian Cataloguing in Publication Data
Adams, Robert J., 1938-
    Horse cop

ISBN 0-9681916-3-0

    1. Adams, Robert J., 1938- --Anecdotes. 2. Royal Canadian Mounted Police–Anecdotes. 3. Canadian wit and humor (English). I. Title.

HV7911.A32A3 1998   C818'.5402   C98-900559-3

Senior Editor: Kelly Hymanyk
Copy Editor: Linda Caldwell
Design, Layout and Production: Kelly Hymanyk
Cover: Rage Studios Inc.
Printing: Jasper Printing

DEDICATION

For my brother Larry Adams, and my brothers-in-laws' Murray Macara, Lester Wall and John Kerster all ex-members of the RCMP and to Canada's finest who trained in the force when horses were held in high esteem and played a very special role in moulding the raw recruit.

CONTENTS

ACKNOWLEDGEMENTS

To my wife Martha, who at times, when I am totally engrossed in writing, must wonder if she has not become a writer's widow.

To my daughter Kelly who has given so much of her time and efforts preparing this book for print. It is to her credit that I am able to develop the many stories that have been so much a part of my life. To Bill, and my granddaughters, Megan and Amy, who have endured the many hours that Kelly has sacrificed to see this book through to its conclusion.

To Larry and Judy Adams for the unbridled enthusiasm and fabulous support they have provided for me in my writing endeavours.

To Sgt. Wayne Carroll, RCMP, "K" Division and Paul Madison with VIA Rail for their knowledgeable help.

INTRODUCTION

Story-telling is an art that has spanned generations. Readers everywhere treasure story-tellers who take them to another place or time. We learn about ourselves and those who came before us when we are engaged in a good story.

Robert Adams continues to share his life experiences with the reader in Horse Cop, his third collection of short stories, when he embarks on his adventure in the RCMP. Upon entering the 'real world' he discovers, as we all do, that many times our perception is not reality. His ability to share with us and allow us to live and laugh at his experiences is the gift of the true story-teller.

MEGAMY PUBLISHING

HORSE COP

THE FLEDGLING

Sleep had not come easy. In fact, I'm not sure I had even slept a wink. The adrenalin was pumping pretty good, and I, Robert J. Adams, a nineteen-year-old country boy, was on a high after receiving my letter of acceptance into the RCMP. I should have been dead tired, but I wasn't. I should have been freezing, but I wasn't. Although I was only wearing my light baseball jacket, I didn't notice the cold as I left the house and walked to work. I was on cloud nine as I drifted along Main Street, for I was one day closer to my dreams. No more mundane office duties for Bobby Adams, assistant forestry clerk. I was destined for bigger things, better times. I was headed for field work, the great outdoors, greener pastures. "Look out world, here I come," I sang out as I floated along. I never even noticed the buildings I passed. Instinct had taken hold of my actions and led me in through the front doors of the Provincial Building. "And a jolly good mornin' to you, sir," I greeted the old caretaker who was huddling inside the huge double doors.

"There's nothin' good about it," he grumbled and gave me a funny look. "Close the door. In case you hadn't noticed, boy, it's colder then the hubs of hell out there."

"It is at that," I chuckled as I raced up the stairs two at a time and sailed into the Edson Forestry office that frosty February morning in 1959. I was just dying to tell someone, anyone, my good news.

"Good morning," I warbled loud and clear as I burst through the door. "And how is everyone on this wonderful day?" Not a single soul answered. I looked around the room, and the only person there besides myself was the old ranger, the one who had taken me to Cadomin for my first summer job. He sat hunkered over a pile of papers on his desk. He had lifted his head slightly and sat there staring at me like I had just come unglued. "And a jolly good morning to you, sir," I crowed as I stamped snow off my shoes before heading for my desk.

The old ranger never moved a muscle, but his eyes followed my every move. He watched as I danced across the room and plunked my butt in my chair. I looked back at him and I gave him a big smile, then I deliberately popped a couple of the snap buttons on my baseball jacket, leaned back and promptly hoisted my feet onto the corner of the desk. "C'mon," I urged him under my breath. "C'mon, ask me." But there was no mental telepathy that passed between us. He just sat there and he watched. Who would give in first, I wondered as I clasped my hands behind my head and smiled.

"Are you okay?" the old ranger finally asked, but in a very cautious tone. After all the delaying, I was starting to get the feeling that the old ranger had been down this road before.

"Me?" I asked. "Why, I've never felt better in my life."

14

"I see," he replied. "You just don't seem to be yourself this morning. I thought maybe you froze a brain cell or two running around with that summer jacket on in the depths of winter. Tell me, son, do you take your baseball jacket off at night, or do you sleep in it?"

Man, but I was dying to tell him my good news. I was going to realize a dream, I was going to be working in a field job. "There will be no more office duties for me," I wanted to shout, but I held my tongue because I wanted him to ask me. To me it was important to be asked. I had to bite my tongue to keep from just blurting it out. "C'mon," I sent him another silent message. "C'mon and ask me why I'm so happy."

"Tell me..." he started to ask the question, then he paused. His eyes got narrow and squinty as he gave me a funny, suspicious look.

"I'll bet the old boy's figured I lost my marbles," I chuckled under my breath as I waited for him to spit it out.

I could almost hear the gears grinding in his head as he searched for the right words. "Well," he finally said, "you're running around half-dressed and you say you ain't froze nothin', I suppose that could be somethin' to be happy about alright. But I don't see that survivin' your own stupidity is cause to come bouncing in here like an ape puttin' your feet on the desk."

"I don't suppose so," I replied. Man, I thought, I'd be retired from the Mounted Police before he got around to asking me one simple little question.

"Well then," he proceeded cautiously. "Did you, per chance, win the Irish Sweepstakes?"

"No," I smiled and shook my head. "I didn't win the Irish Sweepstakes. It's even bigger and better than that."

"Is that so?" he replied. "Now, you tell me, mister, just

what could be better then winning the Irish Sweepstakes?"

I couldn't contain my excitement any longer. "The RCMP," I blurted out. "I'm gonna be a Mountie."

"T'hell you say! The R...C...M...P... You, you're going to be a *horse cop*?" He whistled long and low. "The RCMP," he repeated, like he couldn't believe his ears. "Tell me, young fella," he asked and a sinister grin cracked the old face. "Do the RCMP know about this? Do they know that you, an Assistant Forestry Clerk, are about to grace their great force?"

"You can bet your bottom dollar that they do. In fact, I got my letter yesterday," I replied. "I'm in."

He continued to sit and stare at me for the longest time, but his expression had changed, it was no longer the "when are you going to grow up, kid?" stare, it was sort of a questioning, hurt look. Unwittingly, I had tugged a string and hit a soft spot with the old ranger. "I didn't know...I wasn't even aware that you were contemplating a change," he sort of mumbled when he finally spoke. He had a peculiar sound to his voice. Was he hurt that he hadn't been consulted? Was he hurt because he thought maybe he was the last to know? Maybe he felt hurt that the RCMP would somehow be diminished by my presence. But hurt was there, hurt was definitely in his voice. "I didn't know," he repeated. "For some reason, I can't see you working anywhere but here in this office. Why, I always thought you were happy working up here. You always seemed to be happy. You were happy up here, working with us, weren't you?"

"Sure," it was my turn to mumble. "I guess so. Sure, I guess I was happy all right."

"Why then? What made you decide to change? Was it something we did? Don't you like it here?"

"Was it something we did?" Those words stuck in my head

as my mind wandered back to my year-and-a-half in the position as the assistant clerk in the Edson forest headquarters. Was it something they did? Well, there was no doubt that I far preferred the great outdoors to a seat behind a desk, and I really wanted a job that would let me work outside. I had to admit that being in the office the first summer hadn't been that bad. Not that bad, because there was the pool hall next door. At noon, I often popped over for a quick game of pool. And I played or practiced baseball almost every day. Of course, before and after practice I usually played pool. Occasionally, I took off in the evenings and went fishing or hunting, or I went to the pool hall and played pool. Come to think of it, I suppose it would be safe to say that almost every evening, I could be found at the pool hall shooting a game of pool. Then, there were always the fantastic late-night weenie roasts at the three mile swimming hole on the McLeod river. However, I could usually fit in a game of pool before the weenies beckoned. We rarely played baseball on Saturday, so of course on Saturday I usually opened and closed the pool hall. The pool hall wasn't open on Sundays, so that was the one day I couldn't be found at the pool hall. There was no doubt that I enjoyed shooting pool, and if the truth were known I just about lived at the pool hall. Why, I even had my own personal cue and a place on the rack where I locked it up. What a proud moment in my life getting that lock up on the rack had been.

But, the winter, the winters were different. Sure there was still pool, but there were no baseball games or practices. There was no fishing and even the son of an old poacher like myself now respected the fact that the hunting seasons were closed. The weenie roasts and swimming had ground to a halt when the leaves turned color. With the first frost, my activities had been reduced to two main items, sitting in the office or playing pool. It was the same routine day in and day out. I checked time sheets, expense accounts and processed invoices and the long winter became longer and dragged on and on. In the winter time, I had the office and the pool hall. In a short year and a half, since I had become the assistant clerk, I found myself in a rut. Sitting at my desk all day every day during the long winter weighed awfully heavy and I had a lot of time to think.

One day, I had a vision and I didn't like what I saw. It was lunch time and an old hump-backed man, wearing a weather-beaten frayed Edson Athletics Baseball team jacket, was slouched over a pile of papers at the assistant clerk's desk in the forestry office. It was me, Bobby Adams. I was at least thirty years old. Mom had told me that the walk home was too much for me and that I should start taking a lunch, but the thought of a peanut-butter-and-jam sandwich gagged me. Instead of sitting at my desk eating lunch, I would shoot a game of pool. I could see myself painfully lifting my creaking old bones out from behind the desk. I was barely able to walk, but I shuffled over to the stairs and descended one painful step at a time on knees that popped and cracked. A young fellow paused at the bottom of the stairs, then stepped back and held the door open for me. Once outside, I encountered a couple of young girls. I sucked in my belly as they approached and gave them my best smile. They eyed me cautiously, then stepped gingerly aside and snickered.

It was only a few steps between the Provincial Building and the pool hall and a cool breeze greeted me and wafted over my scalp as I wobbled along. Like Grandfather, the top of my head was as round and smooth as a billiard ball. I couldn't believe it, in ten years of working inside, I had gone

18

bald. I was going to have to be more careful in the future and remember to wear my hat. Nothing could be worse then a cold wind on the old bald pate.

The breeze whistled through the uncontrollable tufts of hair growing from inside my ears. I hunched my shoulders and tugged at the frayed edges of my baseball jacket that now fit snugly around my generous girth. I hobbled on, finally arriving at the pool hall. Some things hadn't changed, I still had the same cue and lock-up that I had rented years earlier. Fumbling with arthritic fingers, curled and stiff from constantly pushing a pen, I cursed the small key as I wrestled with the equally small lock, struggling to remove my cherished personal cue from the rack. Finally, the cue was free, in my hands. Clutching it happily, I turned towards the tables and got a glimpse of the clock. The lunch hour had passed before I was able to take a shot. I was going to be late getting back to the office.

Then and there, I knew I needed a change. There had to be more to life then struggling to get to the pool hall when I was thirty. I longed for days in the fresh air, where there were mountains and trees, sun, wind and stars. I longed for the great outdoors, before it was too late.

"Well," I finally replied. "You know, I really do want to work in the field. On several occasions, I've asked to be sent to a district, any district, to work as an assistant forest officer, but for whatever reason that never materialized. It just seemed to me that the longer I stayed here, the less chance I was going to have to get out."

"Just a minute, young fella," replied the old ranger, getting his hackles up. "I think maybe you're being just a wee bit hasty there. You've had a few chances to get out of the office. Why, I distinctly remember you were on a fire last year. If memory serves me correctly, it was me who sent you out there."

"You're right," I replied humbly. "I was on a fire last year."

How could I ever forget that fire? Oh yes, I had no difficulty whatsoever remembering that fire quite clearly. The fire had been burning northeast of Edson in the hills beyond Spreen's Flats. It had been a very busy, trying period, particularly for the rangers who were otherwise occupied when an order from the fire line came into the office. For me, the day had started out to be quite normal, until the order arrived on my desk. It seemed like the boys on the fire line were working hard and they were a little short on grub. More groceries were needed, and if they arrived yesterday that would not have been too soon. Since none of the rangers were around it was me, the assistant clerk, who received the order from the radio operator. I took it across the street to the Buy-Rite Grocery store and returned to the office. When they called from the store that the order was ready, there just happened to be one person available who could deliver it to the fire camp. That person was none other than the old ranger himself. He had come into the office only to be greeted by a mountain of paper on his desk. The black bags, hanging like large wrinkled prunes under his eyes, told the story. The poor guy looked like he had been working for the past week without sleeping.

"The grocery order for the fire up by Spreen's Flats is ready to go," I advised the old ranger.

"I wasn't aware that there was an order," he replied without looking up from his desk.

"They called it in first thing this morning," I answered. "I took it over to the Buy-Rite to be filled."

"Who gave you the authority to do that?" he asked. "That's a job for the rangers, not a clerk."

"There was no one else here," I protested. "Someone had to do it."

"Hrumph," he grunted. "Well, okay then, if it's done, it's done. I guess there's nothing I can do about it now. But since you're taking so much on yourself, why haven't you called one of the rangers to pick it up?" he mumbled. "Go ahead, call someone. Can't you see I'm busy?"

"I can't. They're all out," I replied. "There's no one here."

"Well young fella, get on the phone and call one of them and tell him to get down here right now. Tell them I said so."

"They're all out on the fire-line," I replied. "There's no one in town."

He sat there, staring at the mountain of paper on his desk. Then he looked up at me, shook his head and returned his eyes to the paper. "I don't suppose you can drive?" he finally asked.

I couldn't believe he was asking me such a question. "Of course I can drive," I stated emphatically. What did he think I was, an invalid or something?

"I don't mean a car," he replied, sounding a little irritated. "Anybody, even a woman, can drive a car. I mean a truck. Can you drive a truck?"

"Of course I can drive a truck. I took driver training two summers in a row with the army cadets in Vernon," I informed him. "I drove big army trucks all over B.C."

"Okay. Okay," he mumbled. "There's a truck parked at the back of the building. The keys are in it. Do you think you can take it over to the store and get the groceries loaded?"

"You bet," I replied, happy for the opportunity to get out of the office and do some real field work. "You want me to take them to the fire, too?"

"No. No, for Pete's sake, no. I don't even want you to take

21

the truck to the store," he grumbled. "But I have no choice. You just get the groceries loaded and stay there. I'll be along shortly. Now leave me be, I've got to find someone who can drive that truck to the fire."

"I can take them," I protested. "I know how to drive a truck, and I know the area, too. We hunt up in that area all the time."

"Just load the groceries, son. I've got enough problems without having to worry about you, too," he replied. The old ranger appeared to age as he talked. He not only looked old, exhausted and cranky, but he sounded old, exhausted and cranky. When he looked at me after making his declaration, I felt like he thought it was my fault he was worn out.

It didn't take long to figure out why the keys were in the truck. It was a dilapidated old beater, on its last legs. Rrrr. Rrrr. Rrrr. The starter complained as the tired old engine barely turned over. It coughed and sputtered several times before it grudgingly kicked in. I tried to shift gears and hoped immediately that no one was watching me. The clashing of metal on metal sounded like I was grinding hamburger. I just about had to jam the clutch right through the floorboards before I got the thing into reverse. The truck reacted immediately, jerking back and almost hitting the side of the building as it burst into the alley. The steering wheel was so loose that I had to spin it like a top before it would catch and the truck would slowly turn. Driving that truck was a painful experience. I suffered and cursed silently, getting that old truck from the back of the Provincial Building, across main street and into the alley behind the Buy-Rite. I suffered more than just a little panic when I backed up to the rear of the store. The brakes were like stepping on a sponge and didn't react immediately and I almost hit the back of the store before the truck stalled and stopped.

I was working up quite a sweat as I tossed boxes and bags of groceries around when the old ranger showed up. He had a second person with him, a friend of mine, a man the same age as myself. A man who had only recently moved to the Edson area.

"Haven't you got this thing loaded yet?" grumbled the old ranger.

"I'm just about finished," I mumbled. I was about to tell him that if the bucket of bolts he gave me was a real truck, I would have been finished a long time ago. But I held my tongue, for there was still a chance, slim as it might be, for me to enjoy an extended field trip.

"You want me to drive this heap?" asked my friend.

"That's right," grunted the old ranger. "As soon as the kid's finished loading the truck, I want you to take it and deliver the groceries to the fire camp out past Spreen's Flats."

"Sure thing. I can do that," he laughed. "Where's Spreen's Flats?"

"Spreen's Flats," repeated the old ranger. "Don't tell me you don't know where Spreen's Flats are. Everybody around here knows where Spreen's Flats are."

"Well, maybe everybody around here does, but I don't. Never heard of them," chuckled my friend.

"Well, lets see now, they're...ah, they're northeast of here," replied the old ranger. "You just have to follow the Bear Lake Road out of town, stay on it until you see a sign. They're easy to find. If you have any trouble once you get out there, just ask anybody, they'll tell you where to go. "

"Gotcha," laughed my friend. "And where do I find the Bear Lake Road?"

The old ranger just stood and looked at his newly acquired

driver as if he couldn't believe what he was hearing. Everyone may not have known where Spreen's Flats were, but everybody in town sure knew where the Bear Lake Road was. He shook his head and sighed. "I guess maybe you better take the kid with you. He says he knows the way. I suppose he can be your swamper in case you have a problem."

"You want me to take little Bobby Adams?" he laughed. "Why doesn't he just take the truck?"

"Because he's just a kid and I want my truck back," snorted the old ranger. "I want to make sure this truck gets out there and back all in one piece. That's why."

"Hey, little Bobby Adams, did you get permission from your mommy to leave town?" roared my friend. The old ranger just grunted and walked away.

"Here, Bob," my friend said. "As long as I'm in charge here, you can drive this thing. I'm just along for the ride."

Man, that's what I call a friend, I thought as I bailed in behind the wheel and ground away on the starter. I was feeling pretty cocky as the grinding of gears echoed throughout the streets of Edson. The truck lurched forward before I let out the clutch. Then the engine coughed, sputtered and backfired and the truck jerked and jumped. In a series of fits and starts, pops and jumps, I coaxed the truck forward. Into the back alley we bounced and jerked. The truck barely missed a telephone pole as I spun the wheel and turned east onto Highway 16. With the help of the loose steering, the truck swung wide, taking up the whole street as I frantically spun the wheel, first one way, then the other. Finally we were rolling along. That the truck was not working properly was of little concern to me. I was sweating like a hog and I was as happy as a lark. Not only was I driving the truck, but now it was I who had a swamper.

The weary old ranger was ahead of us trudging along the side of the Buy-Rite. He was really showing his age as he shuffled along, dragging his feet, his head down. As we rolled toward the intersection, Edson's first and only set of traffic lights changed to red and I was going to have to stop. But first, I thought I'd give the old ranger a little thrill and show him who was driving so I hit the horn and the brakes. At the same time the truck took it upon its own to lurch sharply to the right. In an instant there was more panic. The lights were red, the brakes weren't catching and we were heading straight for the old ranger.

"Whoa! Hit the brakes!" yelled my friend as soon as he saw the truck take a bead on the old ranger. My foot was pumping like a trip hammer on the brake pedal, but to no avail. The spongy brakes were not reacting and the horn, I quickly found out, did not work at all. I spun the wheel to the left, but the truck had its eye on the old ranger's backside. The old ranger was about to get a thrill all right. He was about to meet his maker.

It must have been the instincts of a survivor. For some reason the old ranger glanced over his shoulder. His tired old eyes with bags like wrinkled prunes that a few minutes earlier looked dull instantly took on a shine of sheer panic. Unlike the parts on the truck, when the old ranger kicked into high gear, his parts were working fine. In fact, I couldn't believe my eyes and had to question whether he was as old as I thought. In a flash, the old ranger was, as Dad used to say, "Pickin' 'em up and puttin' em down right smart-like" as he shot ahead of the truck.

I hadn't noticed before, but the old ranger was bow-legged and as those pins started moving rapidly, I thought that if I could get that truck lined up just right, I could probably make it right between his legs. His old knees splayed out like timbers under tremendous pressure each time a foot hit the ground. His eyes were about the size of a cue-ball staring back over his shoulder as he bolted for the end of the building. The truck wasn't slowing down one little bit, but the old ranger was gaining ground as he reached the corner. While I was pumping the brakes and spinning the wheel frantically, praying for either to take hold, he zipped around the corner of the store and out of sight. My knees were knocking like crazy and I was shaking like a leaf when the truck finally rolled to a stop in the middle of the intersection. There was a terrific explosion as the truck backfired once again.

Then I heard the swamper yell, "Green light, get this thing moving, here he comes." I stepped on the gas and let the clutch out so rapidly that the truck bucked and jumped once more. In the rear-view mirror I caught a glimpse of the old ranger racing down the road after us. He was waving his arms and yelling something as we slowly picked up speed and left him behind. "Well, I'd say you certainly got his attention," my friend remarked. He looked back, then leaned out the window and waved to the old ranger.

The old truck was really a pile of junk. It backfired repeatedly, coughed and sputtered as I nursed it out of town and onto the Bear Lake Road. It was a good thing we didn't meet any traffic as that truck used up every inch of the road. I was getting a real good workout as I herded the ruddy thing along and kept it between the ditches. Not only did it steer like a threshing machine, but if I happened to get the speed up to 30 miles per hour, the front end shimmied so bad I thought I was going to chip my teeth. My arms were so tired I thought they were going to fall off. Meanwhile my friend, my swamper, was enjoying the field trip. He laughed and joked as the truck jerked and swayed along. "I'm sure glad it's you driving this heap and not me," he chortled. "I'm gettin' seasick just sitting in here."

After what seemed like an eternity, we passed the last farm house on the road, then turned west onto an old logging road. The smell of smoke was heavy in the air; the fire was getting closer.

Finally, we came across a collection of tents scattered around in the trees. It was the fire camp. We had arrived. I wasn't sure who has happier about our arrival. The crew were extremely happy to see the groceries and willing hands quickly unloaded the truck and tore into the bags and boxes. I was just happy to be able to get out of the truck and rest my aching arms.

"Why don't you take a break and give yourself a rest. If you like, I can drive back," offered my swamper when we were ready to leave.

"I'm fine," I replied. That old truck may have been a bucket of bolts with no horn, spongy brakes and loose steering, but I was the driver. There was no way that I was going to give up or admit that I couldn't handle it. I had been dying to go on a field trip and aching to drive that bloody truck. This was my field trip and I had the truck. I was aching from driving it, but I was going to continue to drive it, even if it killed me.

The drive home was certainly a lot more eventful then the one on the way in. Shortly before we left the logging trail, a rut grabbed the front wheel and threw the old truck to the right. Instinctively I reacted and spun the wheel to the right. For some stupid unknown reason, the steering grabbed, or maybe it was the rut again. In any event the truck suddenly dove to the right and leapt right off the trail. Through the trees the old truck charged, just like a bulldozer. Saplings bent and snapped like match sticks as they fell victim to the fury of the old truck. I covered my face with my arms and stood on the clutch and brake. With the aid of a fairly large poplar tree, the old truck finally jolted to a halt. For a second, it growled and snarled as it strained against the base of the tree, then it sputtered, backfired, wheezed and shuddered. Then all was deathly quiet as its last bit of life was suddenly gone. The old truck was dead.

"You think maybe someone will come by and pick us up?" asked my swamper as he surveyed the treed parking spot from the comfort of the passenger's seat.

"Maybe yes, maybe no," I replied. "I haven't seen another vehicle on this road. How about you?"

"Nope," he responded. "Nothing. Not even a horse and buggy. How far is Edson, anyway?"

"It's a long, beautiful walk," I replied, cheerfully thinking of the trek through the woods that would complete my field trip. I shook my arms to get some feeling back into them as my swamper and I took one last look at the truck. Then we made our way back to the old trail.

"You know, I've been thinking," mused my partner as we picked our way back to the trail. "I think maybe the old ranger was right after all."

"What about?" I asked innocently.

"About you. You know, the more I think about it, the more I realize that he was a pretty sharp old dude. I think I owe him an apology. He was right about you and I shouldn't have let you drive the truck. After all, you are just a kid, you know, and you really don't know anything about driving a truck.... "

"Well," the old ranger spoke up, bringing me back to the

present. "Aren't I right? You've been to the field and more then once, too."

"You're right," I confessed. "But, I see it more as getting out of the office for a day, not going to the field. I really want to go to the field, to work in the field, to get away from the drudgery of office work."

"Humph," grunted the old ranger. "Problem with kids these days is they're never satisfied. They don't know when they've got it good."

"Right," I replied and shifted my feet on the desk to a more comfortable position.

"Well, let me tell you something, mister," growled the old ranger. "It won't be no picnic in the RCMP, neither. You young bucks are all the same, you think that fancy uniform is gonna make you some kind of god. Well, you come back and talk to me in a couple of years time, after you've spent all your time fillin' out reports and filing papers. You let me know just how much field work you get, mister man. You mark my words, you're no different from the rest, you'll be back here and you'll be beggin' for your nice comfy office job."

"Not me," I replied. "I'm outta here. If you're lucky, the next time you see me I'll be zippin' down the highway in my shiny new police cruiser. I'll be the guy drivin', sportin' the new duds, you know, the ones with the nice red coat and the shiny brass buttons."

THE TRUNK

There was no shortage of excitement around the Adams' household as the family prepared for my departure. Mom was determined that I was going to be the best-dressed recruit to hit the RCMP training center in Rockcliffe, and it didn't matter if she had to mortgage the family home to do so. It was to be a shopping spree, the likes of which we had never seen in our lives. My good friend and future brother-in-law Murray, also known as Mac, already a member of the force, proved to be an unending source of information. Mom had no qualms about tapping that reservoir of knowledge.

Mom had called Mac and I together to discuss my needs. Mom had baked a batch of date cookies, two thick oatmeal cookies with dates spread between them, like a large cookie sandwich, for the occasion. We were sitting around the kitchen table planning Bobby's wardrobe for the trip east.

"Bob won't need much in the way of civilian clothes," Mac advised Mom. "He'll get issue clothes as soon as he gets there. When he's on the grounds, he'll wear what the force provides. He'll only need civvies when he leaves the base to go downtown. And he won't be doing that very often," he laughed.

"Why not?" I asked.

"Because you can only leave the barracks on your own time and when you're in training, you don't have much time to call your own. Every time you screw up, you get extra duties and confined to barracks. Knowing you, I'm bettin' that you'll spend most of your spare time confined to barracks." He roared at the little jab.

"If they're gonna give me clothes, then I don't need to take much. I'll just take my jeans, a couple of shirts, some socks, my sneakers and my baseball jacket," I replied.

"Just a minute, young man," Mom interjected. "You'll not be leaving here looking like some waif that nobody loves."

"He'll be okay," Mac assured Mom. "The force will look after him. They give a man everything he needs. He doesn't need to take a whole lot with him."

"Did the force give you the clothes you're wearing right now?" Mom snorted.

"Well no," Mac replied rather sheepishly. "But then, I'm not in training anymore, either."

"I guess they didn't," Mom replied smugly. "Now, let's see, I've made a list of what you'll need. Look at this and tell me what you think. Have I missed anything?"

I took the list Mom handed me and stared in horror. "White shirt! I don't need a white shirt," I protested when I saw the first item at the top of her list. "White shirts are for bankers, they're not for policemen. I'm not wearing any white shirt."

"Aren't you going to Edmonton to be sworn in?" she asked.

31

"Well, yeah," I replied, searching for the right words. "But that's just to be sworn in. I don't need a white shirt to be sworn in."

"When you get sworn in, you'll be dressed properly and that means you'll be wearing a white shirt. And another thing, young man, you're going to have a white shirt on when you leave this house," Mom stated emphatically.

"I suppose the next thing you'll want is for me to wear a necktie, too," I grumbled as Mac laughed.

"Absolutely you'll be wearing a necktie," Mom replied. "You don't wear a white shirt without a necktie. You know that."

"Oh, Mom," I protested and looked back at the list. Sure enough, there it was, number 2 on the list, she had written 'necktie'. Just the thought of it made me squirm. I could feel the tie tightening, just like a noose. "Well, I'll take the white shirt," I mumbled, realizing that if Mom decided I was wearing a white shirt, I was going to be wearing a white shirt. Maybe I could make a better case for dumping the necktie. "But I ain't wearing no stupid necktie. I'll choke to death if I have to wear one of those things."

"And you'll need a new pair of trousers," Mom continued, ignoring both me and the tie. "I thought that black or charcoal would be a good color."

"That's right," Mac chimed in. "I think black would be perfect. It'll go very nicely with your white shirt and tie." Mac seemed to be enjoying himself immensely as he bit into another giant cookie.

"Whatever," I mumbled, thinking about the white shirt and necktie. Who in their right mind could take anybody who wore a white shirt and necktie seriously? I knew I was going to be the laughing stock of Rockcliffe when I showed up with a white shirt and necktie.

"You'll need a new pair of shoes," Mom added.

"I've got a new pair of sneakers," I replied.

Mac laughed again. "You hang in there, son, and stick with them sneakers. If you ask me, everyone should wear a pair of sneakers when they're wearing a white shirt and tie. Oh, and I almost forgot. Sneakers go real good with black pants, especially if you're wearing a white...."

"Put a sock in it, Mac," I mumbled. Mac was not really being much help. In fact, he was starting to grate on my nerves.

"We'll look at some shoes and I guess you'll be needing a new coat, too," Mom sighed. It was like she could hear the old cash register ringing already.

"I've got a new coat," I answered. "What's wrong with my baseball jacket? It's new. I just got it before Christmas."

"You can take it with you if you want," Mom answered. "But you still need a new coat for the trip."

"You betcha," Mac interjected again. "I think that if a man gets all dolled up like little Lord Fauntleroy he should have a coat to suit the occasion."

"You see, Bobby?" Mom smiled happily. "Even Murray thinks you need a new coat."

"Absolutely, a new coat is just the thing you need to hide the white shirt and tie," he roared with laughter. Mac was certainly enjoying himself and the cookies.

"You're no help," Mom informed him. That was the first thing we had agreed on since we sat down, I thought. "First thing tomorrow, we'll go downtown and see what we can find. Oh, I can hardly wait to see you all dressed up. You're going to look so handsome," Mom said, just bursting with pride. "Won't he look handsome, Murray?"

"Oh yeah, he'll look handsome all right," Mac chimed in. "Those instructors will see him coming a mile away. They love to get their hands on a mommy's boy."

"Is that everything we need?" Mom asked, checking the list once more. "Murray, can you think of anything else? Have we missed anything?"

"We've got enough," I grumbled. "At least we got more than I need."

"Mmmmm," Mac mumbled, his mouth full of cookie. "You're gonna need something to pack all them fancy duds in," Mac laughed. "You got something you can pack to take with you?"

"You bet," I replied. "Dad's suitcase. Can I use Dad's suitcase, Mom? He doesn't use it anymore."

"Are you sure you want to use that old thing?" she asked. "You know, it's not in very good shape."

"You bet I do. It's Dad's suitcase. I'll get it," I replied and raced out of the room to retrieve the suitcase my father had used to take his clothes to the bush camps.

I thought Mac was going to fall off his chair, he laughed so hard when I brought the suitcase into the kitchen. It was a large black case. The worn corners and split sides showed quite clearly that it was made of heavy cardboard. Two old leather belts were strapped around near the ends to keep it together. "I guess it's not in such good shape, is it?" I mumbled, looking at Mac who was laughing like a hyena.

"Put that old thing away," Mom replied. "We'll get you a new one."

"A trunk," Mac sputtered through his fits of laughter. "A

suitcase is no good. It'll never hold all his gear. Get him a good trunk."

Saturday was our big shopping day. With me in tow, Mom hit all the stores in Edson, both of them. Mom picked out the clothes she had decided on. First item on the list was the white shirt. I grumbled constantly as Mom handed me one shirt after the other, trying to find one that both the neck and sleeves fit. "Have you ever noticed that he's got a funny build? It seems to me like he's got pretty long arms for a fella his size," observed the frustrated clerk at the clothing store. It seemed that the sleeves on every shirt he brought out stopped just short of my wrists. "Did you ever notice how long his arms are, Mrs. Adams?" he asked.

The clerk had not paid close attention to Mom when he made the first remark. If he had, he certainly wouldn't have made the second.

"There's nothing wrong with his arms," Mom snorted indignantly. "It's too bad that they don't have anything in here that fits a normal person," she declared as she hustled me out the door. Mom was fuming as we trundled off down the street to the next store. If the second and last store in town didn't have a white shirt that fit a normal kid, with a healthy reach, I figured we could be out of business pretty fast. I chuckled when I thought of the white shirt being only a distant memory. But my luck did not hold. "Bobby needs a man's shirt," Mom advised the clerk. "His arms are fully developed, you know?"

"Certainly, Mrs. Adams," replied the very astute clerk and promptly produced a white shirt. "I think it's a perfect fit," he replied confidently. "Don't you think so, Mrs. Adams?"

"What do you think, Bobby?" Mom asked. "You're the one that has to wear it."

"I think it's about the same as the others," I replied, hoping to rid myself of the thing.

"Good," Mom replied. "I think it fits just fine. Now, we also need a pair of black or charcoal trousers."

"What size?" asked the clerk, looking at me.

"I don't know," I replied. "Big enough to fit me, I guess."

"That's no problem if you don't know your size," he sang out. "I'll just measure you up." He whipped the tape measure from around his neck. "Hold your arms up please," he instructed. I felt like a fool when he wrapped his arms around me and wrestled with the tape before announcing. "Waist twenty-eight inches." But I really got alarmed when he got down on his knees in front of me and ran one hand up the inside of my legs, all the way to the crotch.

"Hold on now," I shouted. "That'll be enough of that."

"If I'm to fit you properly, I have to measure your inseam, Bobby," he responded, sounding just a little overly friendly. After the embarrassing experience, he was able to produce a pair of charcoal trousers and a tie that satisfied Mom.

"What kind of overcoat would you like?" Mom asked.

"I don't care," I replied. "As long as it covers this white shirt and tie."

"I have just the thing," replied the clerk, who couldn't believe his good luck. By this time I was sure he had little dollar signs dancing around in his eyes. He moved swiftly to another corner of the store and brought out a very nice light grey-colored coat. "I would recommend this three-quarter-length car-coat. It's the in thing, very much in style," he nodded knowingly. "Here Bobby, try it on," he said, holding it for me. The Bobby's were starting to get on my nerves. I had always been Bob to this guy, but now in front of Mom, I was suddenly Bobby.

I slipped my arms into the sleeves, buttoned the coat and walked over to the mirror. Not bad, I thought as I admired the image staring back at me. "It's perfect," he warbled. "Oh, it just fits like a glove. Isn't it a perfect fit, Mrs. Adams?"

"Yes. I think it fits very nice," Mom replied. "How do you like it, Bobby?"

"It doesn't hide the white shirt," I informed him. "I want something that hides the white shirt and the necktie."

"A scarf," he countered quickly. "What you need is a scarf." He whipped over to another counter and plucked a plaid scarf off so fast it would make your head spin. Then he was back and wrapping that thing around my neck and tucking it in under the lapels. "There you are, Bob. Look in the mirror. What do you see? No shirt and no necktie." He smiled smugly, quite proud of his accomplishment.

"Bobby needs a pair of oxfords, too," Mom informed him.

"I have a very nice brown pair," replied the clerk.

"If I have to wear oxfords, I want a black pair."

"I have a very nice pair of black oxfords," he replied without missing a beat and in a second produced a shoe box with the oxfords. His nimble fingers were flying as he threaded the laces through the eyes and with the aid of a shoe horn, crammed them on my feet. "There. How do they feel, Bobby?" he asked.

"They're a little tight," I complained. "They hurt my heels right here." I pointed to the top of the oxford where the stiff leather bit into my ankle.

"That's normal for new shoes," he assured me. "They just have to be worn in. You won't notice it after a few days."

"You look so handsome," Mom purred happily as I stood before her all dressed up in my brand-new duds. "Now we have to go and get you a trunk," Mom stated.

"One moment, please, Mrs. Adams," interjected the clerk. "If I may be so bold as to make a suggestion, I have a little something here that I think is just the thing to complete Bobby's outfit."

"What would that be?" Mom asked.

"Well, I was thinking that a nice sports coat would complete his wardrobe and I just happen to have one that I think will be perfect." Before Mom could reply he scooted into the back and came out with a black and white checkered sports coat. "Here we are, we just received this coat," he announced proudly.

"Oh my goodness, yes! Try it on, Bobby," Mom urged me. She was so excited, she was almost out of breath. "I can't wait to see it on you." Reluctantly I shed my new car-coat and donned the black and white job. "Oh, Bobby, I knew it. The moment I saw that coat, I knew it was meant for you," she cooed. "Just the other day, I saw a picture of Marlon Brando and he was wearing a coat just like that and he looked just like you." Mom stepped back to admire me, then without warning, "Don't you think that Marlon Brando looks just like Bobby?" she asked the clerk. I could have crawled into a hole, I felt so embarrassed.

"Marlon Brando?" asked the surprised clerk as he, too, took a step back to see what he had missed. "Oh...yeah," he stammered, trying to find the right words, but he recovered beautifully. "I sure do, Mrs. Adams," he suddenly blurted out happily as more dollar signs danced around.

"Can we go and get a trunk now?" I asked, just wanting to get away.

"In a minute. I just want to look at you for a while longer," she replied. "It's not every day that I get to see you all dolled up."

With the new clothes, including the Marlon Brando coat, wrapped and carefully stored in a couple of shopping bags, we began our search of Edson for a good trunk, but soon discovered there was not a trunk to be had that met with our criteria. We were undeterred and that evening, the search continued. This time, it was around the kitchen table as we thumbed our way through both the Eaton's and Simpson's catalogues looking for the ideal trunk. There were a few displayed on the pages and after a considerable amount of deliberation and some timely suggestions from Mac, we reached a decision. A trunk large enough to hold all the gear that a policeman had to ship around the country was ordered from the Eaton's catalogue.

When I picked it up at the CN freight office, I had this nagging feeling that the big trunk was one step ahead of me, having already made its first trip, albeit empty, to Edson.

Finally the great day arrived. The day I had been waiting for. The day I left Edson. As Mom had so accurately predicted, I was all dressed up in my brand-new duds, complete with white shirt and necktie. The last thing I did before my brother Larry and I lugged the new trunk outside was to carefully pack my belongings. Very carefully I folded my extra pair of pants and laid them on one side. My shirts were folded and laid on top of the pants. On the other side I carefully placed my baseball jacket. In between the two I laid out my socks, underwear and my almost-new sneakers. I stood and gazed into the depths of the trunk, way down to the bottom where my clothes lay. Man, it was a big trunk, I thought. There was more bottom showing than clothes. Grandfather arrived just as we were finishing the packing. "I just stopped by to wish you luck, boy," Grandfather warbled.

"After all, I couldn't let this boy leave town without saying goodby. You know, it's not every day that a grandson of mine leaves home to become a *horse cop*," he laughed and slapped me on the back. "Here boy, can I help you?" he asked.

"We're all finished packing, Grandfather," Larry replied. "I'll close the lid and fasten 'er down, Rob."

"You're all finished?" Grandfather asked as he took a curious look into the depths of the trunk. "But the trunk is almost empty. You can put a whole lot more in there, boy," he observed.

"That's all I need," I replied.

"Well, boy, if that's all you need, you sure won't be needing that big trunk. What say I just take it off your hands, then. What do you want for it, boy?" he asked, pulling out his wallet. Grandfather was never one to let a good bargain pass.

"It's not for sale," I replied. "Let's get this thing out of here before he does," I mentioned to Larry.

"Careful we don't tilt 'er," Larry cautioned, as we carried the trunk through the door and prepared to hoist it into the trunk of the car.

"Why?" I asked, like a dummy.

"We don't want everything in there to shift. Else we might have to unpack 'er and start all over again," he laughed.

"Sure thing," I laughed, thinking that my meager belongings had to be swimming in the empty interior.

Then it was time to say goodby. My youngest sister Judy had gone to school, but Dad was there. I looked up at him standing at the top of the back step. He had to work and would not be accompanying me to Edmonton. Man, I just stood beside the car and looked at him. I didn't know what to say. I didn't know how you said goodby to your father. If it had been Mom, there would have been no problem. A big hug, a loving kiss and a few tender 'I love you's'. Tears would be shed and then I'd be gone. But how did I say goodby to Dad? None of the Mom things seemed to be appropriate. It was an awkward moment as I climbed the steps. Man, what a useless feeling. I just stood there, speechless.

"S'long, Bob," he said in his quiet easy-going manner. "You take care of yourself now, son." Then he held out his hand. The s'long was the same as I had heard him say to Mom so many times before when he left to work in the bush camps. I shook his hand. As I stood there shaking his hand, I noticed that he had not shaved and he looked old and tired. Somehow, the handshake did not seem to be appropriate. Something was missing. Before I realized what was happening, I did the unmanly thing and probably scared ten years of life out of my father. I suddenly reached out and wrapped my arms around him and gave him a big hug. I tried to say goodby, or s'long, anything, but the words wouldn't come. My eyes were brimming with tears as I turned and fled to the car. I never said goodby to my father.

I was having mixed feelings, not the least of which was my aching feet, as I drove the '53 Meteor out onto the highway and sped away, toward the rest of my life. Mom, Larry and my sister Gwen accompanied me on the first leg of my trip, the swearing-in ceremonies in Edmonton. The car was filled with emotions, excitement and sadness, everyone alone with their own thoughts. Man, but we were an awfully quiet bunch in that car as we drove east on Highway 16.

My first night away from home was spent at the Royal George Hotel in Edmonton. I was in a pretty jovial mood. I laughed and joked the whole time. I found every little thing to be exceptionally humorous, while Mom, Gwen and Larry went through the motions. I was so caught up in my own importance that I completely missed the little things, the important things. I missed the sadness in the eyes of my mother. I missed the downcast look of my sister. I missed the forlorn look on my brother's face. I missed the emptiness they were feeling. They were the ones remaining behind and they, more than I, recognized the passing of an era. There was little sleep that night, but for each of us there was an entirely different reason.

First thing the next morning, sporting my new duds and looking as spiffy as an altar boy, I swore an oath. While my family waited outside in the car, I became a member of the Royal Canadian Mounted Police.

I met two others that morning. They were introduced as two of my new troop mates. I was relieved and felt much more reassured when I noticed that they, too, were dressed to the nines. One even had on a white shirt and necktie. We could have been brothers, I thought.

When we were ready to leave "K" Division headquarters, I noticed that the three of us even had on the same coats, right down to the color. As I walked out of the building with my new troop mates, I don't mind saying that I was feeling pretty cocky. I introduced them to my family and nudged Mom. "Look," I whispered to her. "They've got car-coats the same as me. We'll have to be careful we don't get them mixed up."

"No," she replied. "That shouldn't be a problem. Their coats are a little darker than yours. See, yours is much whiter, and you have only one button on the sleeve. They have two. Could I get you boys to stand together for a picture?" Mom asked.

We were three pretty cool dudes and casually leaned against the building. While Mom was aiming the camera, I happened to look down. The guy next to me did have two buttons on his sleeve, just like Mom said. Then, I noticed more than just the buttons. I noticed that their three-quarter-length car-coats were about six inches longer then mine. But, the worst was yet to come. I was staring down, looking at my wrists, hanging about an inch below the bottom of the sleeve, while my troop mate's sleeves came onto their hands, just above the knuckles. Then I realized that my brand-new car-coat was not quite 'the in thing' that the sales clerk had made it out to be.

Man, but my feet were killing me as I felt the air go out of my sails as I realized that the coat would hide the shirt and tie, but nothing was going to hide the shortcomings of the coat. I tried everything I could think of to get my hands up higher into the sleeves. The best luck I had was to scrunch my shoulders up, but after a while, I started to get a stiff neck. Finally I relented, my shoulders sagged and my hands popped clear of the sleeves. Maybe the first sales clerk was right, I thought. Maybe I was a misfit.

Together, my troop mates and I, dressed in my new car-coat with all its shortcomings, would be taking the train, traveling across Canada, all the way to Rockcliffe, Ontario. To a country boy who used to travel all the way from Edson to Wildwood to spend a week of summer holidays, Rockcliffe was a world away. At the railway station, I forgot about the shirt and tie. I even forgot about the coat. I was caught up in the excitement of my new adventure. I could hardly contain myself as I said my farewells to my family. I think my eyes were the only dry ones in the tearful farewell.

The conductor had placed a little stool at the bottom of the steps to help people on. I eagerly bounded onto the stool and up the steps when the conductor called, "All aboard". I waited while he collected his stool and climbed on board. I watched while he dropped a floor piece in place and closed the gate. I stood there, leaning out of the doorway over the gate waving goodby as the train pulled out of the station. I was on my way to bigger and better things. There would be no more mundane office jobs for me.

DO NOT FLUSH WHILE TRAIN IS IN THE STATION

I was an old hand when it came to train travel. For as far back as I could remember, the train had played a big part in my extensive travel schedule. I remember as a lad, living in Hornbeck, catching the passenger trains with Mom and my brother and sisters. We made that twelve-mile trip from Hornbeck to Edson many times. After we moved to Edson and lived on the stump farm, I had even taken the train, by myself, all the way to Wildwood, fifty miles to the east. There I would spend a week of my summer holidays with my aunt. Why, on two separate occasions, I had even traveled from Edson to Vernon, B.C. to attend the Army Cadet Training Camp. Oh yes, train travel was not new to me. I knew trains and I knew my way around them pretty good. I was a man of the world and had been on more than my fair share of train trips.

The steam engine huffed and puffed and slowly the train pulled away from the station. I hung out over the half-opened door and waved to Mom and Gwen and Larry until the train followed a curve and they disappeared from sight. I watched as the station, the last connection to my family, finally disappeared in the distance, then I left my post at the half-opened door. It was time to check out the car I'd be traveling in for the next few days. With any luck, I'd get a seat on the good side, the good side being a seat by the window on the side of the train where all the good things to see were. During my travels, I had discovered that the good things to see were always being pointed out by people on the other side of the train. I often found myself jumping up and down like a yo-yo trying to look over their shoulders and past their heads. Then, I realized that being the last one in through the door was not such a brilliant move. I was going to have to take whatever seat was left. Now I could only hope there was still a good seat. I preferred a seat by the window where I could look forward toward the engine and see what was coming. I could spend my whole trip in a seat by the window where I could watch the trees and the rivers. I just loved to sit and watch the country roll by.

With my first couple of steps, I got another message that was in no way related to a good seat. The message was more deep-rooted than that. It came from my feet. Standing at the door hadn't done my poor feet any good. My blisters were having their own little war with my new pair of shoes. Each blister was fighting for space and room to expand in the unforgiving hard leather shoes. Every little movement sent a thousand searing pains shooting through my feet. As I looked down at my aching feet, I realized I had made a terrible mistake. The only clothes I had with me were the clothes on my back. Everything else I owned was tucked away in my trunk. Man, I was going to have to suffer through the next few days with my new pants, white shirt and the pinchy, rough pieces of leather the man had sold me for shoes. I moaned and cursed my own stupidity for not having thought to bring a change of clothes and my comfortable sneakers with me.

As soon as I walked into the car, I knew I had taken a wrong turn or the conductor had made some sort of mistake and put me on the wrong car. Every train I had ever been on had an aisle down the center and two rows of seats on either side. On this car, I found myself walking down this narrow corridor, between a couple of sets of berths. The seats here looked far more comfortable then those in the day cars and for the moment, I forgot about my feet.

A berth was better then I hoped for and since I was going to be on the train for a couple of days, it only made sense that I would have a berth. However, I quickly discovered that I was not going to get a berth-seat facing forward, backwards, by the window or the corridor. I checked again and sure enough, every seat was already occupied. Undaunted, I followed the corridor as it zigzagged along. I hadn't even gotten a third of the way down the car when a zig took me to the right and there I was, on the edge of the car, right up against the windows. On the other side of the corridor was a solid wall with half-a-dozen doorways. "I'm in the wrong car," I mumbled out loud. "That stupid conductor must have made a mistake." I turned on my sore heel to go back the way I came. I'm not sure who was more surprised by my sudden change of directions, me or the stupid conductor. I had been so intent on finding a good seat that I hadn't realized he had followed me into the car and was hot on my blistering heels. As I turned, I hit him with a solid body check. He bounced off the wall and window, then just missed kicking me with the biggest shoes I had ever seen on a man before falling through a doorway on the other side of the corridor.

"I'm not the conductor, I'm the porter. Is there something

47

wrong, sir?" wheezed the unhappy porter, a huge black man who hastily extracted himself from the doorway and straightened his uniform as he gasped to regain his breath.

"Yeah, I think so," I replied, trying to get a better look at the inside of the room. I could definitely see two chairs and was wondering what else there may be. "I think you must have put me in the wrong car. There's no seats in here."

"Could I see your ticket, please?" he asked as he finished rearranging his coat and resetting his cap.

I dug into my pocket, fished out my ticket and handed it to him. "I'm in the wrong place, aren't I?" I questioned him as the train started to pick up speed and my confidence about train travel suddenly started to wane.

"No sir," he replied happily. "You're in the right place and if I may say so, you're also in the right hands. I'm your porter and if there's anything I can do for you, you just ask. But first, you come right this way and I'll show you to your quarters."

"Yeah," I replied, not able to hide my surprise at this revelation. "You mean I got a porter and I got quarters, too?"

"Yes sir, you sure do. Right this way," he replied and motioned for me to start down the narrow corridor ahead of him.

"What about this room?" I asked, trying to get a little better look inside the opening he had just pulled himself out of. "This room looks fine to me and it's empty. I think this room would be fine."

"No, sir, that's not your room. That's a bedroom. Bedrooms are for two people. Your room is at the other end of the car." Again he motioned for me to lead the way.

"I'm sure if I had a good look around this train, I could find someone to share this 'bedroom' with," I kidded.

"Please move forward," he replied brusquely, not taking

kindly to my sense of humor. We walked down the corridor and took a zag to the left. I reached the door at the end of the car and thought that I was going to lead the way right out of the car before he called out. "This here's your room, sir," he said, holding a curtain back to give me a look into another room.

I really thought he had to be kidding. "You mean I haveta sleep in here? This is a bathroom?" I complained as I looked at a small stainless steel sink and a toilet bowl sitting just inside the door. "I'm not sleepin' in no bathroom," I advised him in no uncertain terms. "This is your roomette, sir," chuckled the porter, obviously a little more then amused at my lack of knowledge. "Is this your first time on the train?" he asked and gave me a condescending smile.

Ignoring his question, I pushed past him, through the curtains and into the room. My roomette was one dinky little room all right. It had a sink, a toilet bowl and one arm chair. "But, there's no bed in this here roomette," I complained as I started to have some grave thoughts about my latest choice of careers. "Where do you expect me to sleep, in the chair?" I mumbled.

"Don't you worry none about the bed, sir," he smiled. "Come nightfall, you'll have a bed all right and I'll be here to make it up for you."

"Yeah, you're kidding me?" I replied. I looked around the room, at the toilet, at the chair, at the sink, at the small cramped little space. "And just how are you gonna get a bed in here? Where are you gonna throw the other stuff?"

"Your bed's already here, sir," he replied, grinning from ear to ear. "It's in the wall right behind your chair. All's we do is unhook it and drop it down over the chair and the toilet."

"Is that so?" I replied and looked up at the wall behind the chair. Sure enough, there was a hook up there. Maybe things weren't as bleak as they seemed. "Well now, I guess that's not such a bad deal then, is it?" I chuckled and congratulated myself. Not only do I get a private room, a biffy and a sink, but I also got a porter and he's gonna make my bed, too. I knew at that moment that I had made the right decision when I joined the force. They certainly knew how to treat a man. "Hey, things are really starting to look up, aren't they?" I crowed as I plunked my butt in the comfy arm chair and looked out the window at Edmonton passing before my very eyes. Without thinking, I put my feet up on top of the toilet seat.

"If you don't mind, sir," stated a somewhat agitated porter and he pointed toward the toilet and my feet.

"What?" I replied and then I noticed a little sign on the wall behind the toilet.

"DO NOT FLUSH WHILE TRAIN
IS IN THE STATION"

"Oh, I see, you want me to flush the toilet with my foot?"

"No! I would like you to take you shoes off before putting your feet on the toilet seat."

"Why's that?" I asked. "It makes a perfect footstool."

"Manners, sir, and it's not a footstool."

"Okay, no problem," I chuckled and kicked the shoes off onto the floor. "Oh, man, does that feel good on my blisters," I moaned. "How's that?" I asked. "Are you satisfied?"

"Well, it's a little better, but instead of cluttering up your room, you might want to use the closet we provide for your shoes." He grunted and pointed to a little door in the wall above the sink.

I got up and stepped over to the wall. I reached up and turned the handle and sure enough there was a little cubbyhole up there. I picked up my shoes and placed them inside. "How about that, a perfect fit."

"Oh, that's good, very good," he replied. "Will there be anything else?"

"Not that I can think of."

"Your meals will be served in the dining car. It's straight ahead in the next car."

"Well now," I chuckled. Suddenly I felt this hunger pang gnawing away at my belly. "One thing I'm good at is eatin' and I can eat anything at any time. So it must be time to dine. You just lead the way, my friend." I was certainly glad that he had mentioned food.

"No sir, not right now," he interjected. "You eat your meals at mealtime. I'll call you when supper is being served."

"Well, you just tell the cook to hurry it up," I trumpeted loudly. "You tell him that he's got one hungry young man back here."

"Oh, yes sir," he laughed, then pulled the curtains shut. "Yes sir, I'll be sure to tell the cook." I heard his voice grow faint as he walked away.

"Hey, this is great," I sang out. In fact it was more than I had ever dreamed of. I sat back on the nice plush chair. I put my feet, with socks on only, back on the toilet seat. I put my hands behind my head and leaned back. I looked out the window. There were fewer buildings now, Edmonton was being left behind. I noticed that the train was slowing down. I moved toward the window and pushed up tight against it. I strained my eyes looking forward to see why. Why were we stopping so soon, I wondered? Ahead, I could see what appeared to be a gully, but as the train slowed and drew closer the gully became a valley. The valley of the North Saskatchewan River slowly emerged, then dropped away below us. I looked down on the frozen surface of the river as the train inched its way over the trestle.

As the train crawled along, I again looked at the little sign behind the toilet. Well, I thought, we're not in a station now. I lifted the lid and looked inside the bowl. Except for the little metal flap at the bottom, it didn't look any different from any other toilet until I flushed it. As the water whirled around and flowed out, I could see right through, through the toilet seat, through the white porcelain bowl and through the little straight pipe to the outside world. I could see the railroad ties and the gaps between them as they slowly passed below. Water, toilet water was splashing off them and dropping through on its way to the ice-covered river below. Neat, I thought, as I lowered the lid and returned to my seat and the broader view.

The train's slower speed had only been temporary, for once across the trestle the train again sped up and raced over the prairie, heading for Rockcliffe. Once more I flushed the toilet and looked through the hole at the ties that were now a blur, like someone flipping through a deck of cards as they whistled past. Then I sat back and rested my blistered feet on the toilet seat.

That evening, after I had dined with my new troop mates, we sat and talked, swapped war stories and joked, then I returned to my quarters. I had to check to make sure that I was in the right place, for the curtain was now zipped right down the middle. When I opened it, I was really surprised, for there in front of me, just as the porter had promised, was my bed. My roomette was almost wall-to-wall bed. To enter my room, I had to crawl onto the bed, then turn around and zip the curtains shut. Once again, I was alone in the privacy of my roomette. Man, but this was great. I took off my shoes and placed them in the little cubbyhole above the sink and took off my clothes. Too much had happened in the past few days and I was too worked up to sleep. Then, I did something that I had never done at home, would never have dreamed of doing in a bedroom shared with my brother and often entered by Mom without any advance warning. As the distance between me and home increased, I lay in the buff, on top of my comfortable bed. Man, what a life it was to be so free that I could lay buck-naked on top of the bed, look out through the big window and watch the world roll past.

As the train raced through the night, across the Canadian prairie, I had lots of time to think, to dream, to dream of the finer things to come. I could see myself as a member of Canada's finest. Oh, but I cut a mean swath as I strutted about dressed in full uniform. In my scarlet tunic, my Stetson tilted slightly to just the right angle on my head, my riding breeches with the bright yellow stripe running down the side of the leg to the top of the riding boots and the spurs strapped to each boot, with my six-shooter strapped on my hip, I was ready for whatever challenges I encountered. I could just picture myself, methodically working my way through a very trying investigation, racing to the aid of an injured or lost person or working undercover. I bet I could find the moonshiners. With my knowledge of the woods, I'd be invaluable in hunting out shiners and destroying stills.

Where would I be stationed to fight all this crime and evil, I wondered? Would I be sent back out west to work on the flat lands that I was now traveling through? Would I be back at this very location? No, the bald-headed prairies were probably too close to home. Mac had told me they wouldn't send me back to where I came from, and anyway, there had to be better places to work then on the prairie. Maybe I would be transferred east, to the Maritimes. The Maritimes would be nice, but, the more I thought about them, the more I realized they were a long way from home. If I went to the Maritimes, I might never see my family again. What about Ontario? What about Quebec? Would I end up in Upper or Lower Canada? What was the possibility? Well, I didn't speak French, so Quebec was probably out of the question. If Mac had been right, and both Quebec and Ontario had provincial police forces, they most likely didn't warrant much thought.

Then of course, there was the beautiful province to the west, British Columbia, yeah, now that was where I wanted to go. It had everything. Mountains, there were tons of mountains. Trees, well Dad, the logger in the family had spent some time in British Columbia and he always said, "the biggest and tallest trees in Canada grow in British Columbia". Hunting and fishing, oh yeah, I could hunt deer, moose and elk and I could fish salmon every day of the year. There was no doubt about it, the province to the west had it all and it was close to home. Oh yes, that's where I wanted to go all right, to British Columbia. I could hardly wait to get to British Columbia.

Somewhere between dreaming of British Columbia and seeing a vision of a dashing young man from Alberta, all decked out in a red tunic, I fell asleep. The vision was so real I could just about feel it. I was the handsome young man. I could see myself patrolling in my shiny black cruiser, parking it for all to see, then making my rounds. Dressed to the nine's in my dazzling uniform, I was strutting along a boardwalk. In the background was the beautiful blue Pacific Ocean. I was fighting off hordes of beautiful girls who were absolutely wild about the scarlet tunic when my dreams were so rudely shattered. It was a wake-up call from mother nature.

When I rose to respond to mother nature, I was quickly

reminded that the bed, in the down position, covered the biffy. Before answering the call the bed would have to be returned to the upright position. I wriggled my way into the only available space, a small area between the bed and the curtains hanging in the doorway. In this precarious position, there was not enough room to lift the bed. I squirmed around until I got hold of the zipper and lifted it just a bit, opening my door curtain enough to get my bottom out into the corridor so I could lift the bed to the upright position. But, there was too much of me left in the little roomette and I repeatedly lifted the zipper a couple more inches and stuck a little more of my bottom into the corridor. Each time I tried to hoist the bed from the floor to the wall I found I needed a little more room. Finally, I had the right combination, the zipper was right to the top of the curtain and my bare bottom along with the rest of me was standing in the corridor. Not a good idea when you sleep in the buff. I quickly realized that while my bed was going up, my bare butt was going out. Out into the corridor for anyone to see.

As the bed went up, my butt came in and the zipper finally came down. With the bed finally locked into place in the upright position and the zipper on the curtains pulled all the way down, I plunked myself down on the throne. I sat alone in my private quarters, on my private throne looking back, out the window into the long endless prairie night. I was looking back to where I had come from. The clackety-clack of the steel wheels on the steel tracks were the only sounds that broke the silence. The train was somewhere in eastern Alberta or western Saskatchewan, I didn't know where, but I sat in the darkness of my roomette and gazed into the long night. It was a clear night, the moon and stars reflecting off the blanket of snow that covered the prairie. On this clear night, I felt like I could see to the ends of the earth. I gazed back across the vast prairie, upon mile after mile of fields, treeless fields. Here and there, near and far, scattered across the countryside the lights shone brightly. They were probably lighting up farm yards. Yard lights, that was something we never had on the stump farm. As I watched the light reflecting off the snow-covered fields, I couldn't help but think back. Back to the stump farm on a winter's night when the only light reflecting on the snow was cast from the kerosene lantern hanging in the kitchen window. A glimpse of light suddenly danced across a huge snow drift and I had to chuckle. For a moment, I thought of Grandfather and the dancing flames on the snow as he heated up the outdoor biffy by burning paper in the hole. I wondered where the old fox was right now, probably sound asleep.

A set of car lights on a lonely country road brought a strange feeling to the pit of my stomach. Had Mom, Larry and Gwen got home safely after dropping me off? I felt a twinge of guilt as I remembered who I had left behind, for in my total preoccupation with myself and my venture I had forgotten everyone at home. Man, I thought, smacking myself on the forehead, I hope that's not a sign of things to come.

Suddenly, I was yanked back to the present as the inside of my quarters were lit up like a town square. I looked out the window and realized the train had slowed and we were passing by a street lamp. The train was passing through a small farming community. I started to stand up then remembered I was buck naked and quickly dropped back onto the throne. As the train passed by the station, a lone body was standing on the platform. He waved and smiled. I hesitated, then realized he didn't know what I was doing or that I was naked, I waved back. How about that, I chuckled, here I am sitting on the throne waving to people and no one but me knows I'm

56

buck naked. It was a good thing I had tested the toilet earlier. If I had flushed at the station, that poor fella could have gotten the surprise of his life.

I slipped into my pants and stepped out into the corridor to once more lower my bed. Laying on the top of the bed I dozed and it did not take long for the dreams of glory and grandeur to return. But again I was awakened, this time by a noise that I was sure came from inside my roomette. I lay very still and listened, then suddenly the sounds of the traveling train thundered throughout the car as a door opened, then slammed shut. Now I was wide awake, for I knew what those sounds were, someone was moving between the cars. I quickly unzipped my curtain door and stuck my head into the corridor. There was no one there, all was quiet and peaceful as the train slept. But I knew I had heard something and as I was surveying the empty corridor, I noticed a small door high on the wall of the roomette across from mine. That's funny, I thought, I hadn't noticed that before and I absentmindedly looked up on my wall. Oh no, I thought as I stared at the wall, I have one of those little doors too. I hadn't seen it before, but I got a real bad feeling, was that the noise I heard? Did that little door on the outside wall lead to the little cubbyhole where my shoes were? I jumped out into the corridor and yanked the little door open. It was a little cubbyhole, just like the one on the inside of the roomette and it was empty. I charged back through the curtain, onto my bed and pulled the door open on my little cubbyhole. I stared into the empty space, and through the opening from the door on the outside wall. My brand-new oxfords were gone. My oxfords had been stolen, right from over my nose.

Immediately I thought of the porter. He did it, I knew it. It was the porter who told me to put my shoes up there. I just knew that at that very minute he was hiding somewhere trying on my shoes. Without thinking, I jumped back out into the corridor and searched both ways, but there was no one about. In fact, there was no sound save that of the wheels, the clackety-clack of the railway track. Oh, man, but I had a sick feeling in the pit of my stomach as I returned to my little roomette. What was I going to do? I had no shoes. I was going to have to walk around barefooted. That wouldn't be bad on the train, but what about when I had to get off? What was I going to do in Ottawa? My sneakers and everything else I owned was in my trunk.

"My trunk," I called out as I suddenly realized I didn't have my trunk and to make matters worse, I didn't even know where it was. My trunk, like me, was alone and hopefully it was somewhere on the train. What if my trunk hadn't been loaded on the train? My mind was starting to play little tricks with me and I could just see some guy back at the station picking it up and thinking it was there by mistake. With my few belongings in it, I had to admit that it felt empty, it would be easy for somebody to think it had been abandoned. Would he put it on the train, or take it home with him? My poor clothes, where were they and my almost new sneakers, were they alone in the baggage car or in somebody's house? Man, it was a sad day, I hadn't even been away from Mom for a whole day, and already somebody had stolen my shoes and my trunk was probably gone, too.

I was one sick-looking specimen, feeling real sorry for myself when I finally dragged my carcass out of bed in the morning. By the time I backed my butt out of the roomette and stepped into the aisle, I had all my clothes on except my shoes. The first face I saw was that of the porter. He was wearing a big friendly smile. "Mornin', sir," he greeted me.

"Did you sleep well?"

"No," I mumbled as I looked my prime suspect square in the eyes. Why would he be smiling like that, I wondered? Because he just stole your shoes, you dummy, I told myself. Wouldn't you be smiling if you just got yourself a brand-new pair of oxfords that you didn't have to pay for? I paused and sized him up; could I detect just a trace of a sinister smile on that face? I wondered.

"Well, sir, maybe what you need is a good breakfast," he replied cheerfully.

"I don't feel so hungry," I replied, eyeing him suspiciously. I couldn't get my mind off the fact that I had been a policeman for less then a day and in that short time, someone, probably this grinner standing in front of me, had stolen my shoes.

"You get along now and have yourself some breakfast," he replied. "I'm sure you'll feel a lot better after you've had something to eat."

"I doubt it," I mumbled. I never took my eyes off him as I limped past him. He never took his eyes off me, either. I was just about to take the zag in the aisle when he called out.

"Excuse me," the porter called out. He was having quite a chuckle when he added "we don't like you to put your shoes on the toilet seat, but we do allow you to wear them to breakfast."

"That's a good one," I replied. "You probably already know that somebody stole them last night."

"They did what?" he replied, sounding shocked. The big smile on his face disappeared like he had been hit with a hammer. "Are you sure, sir?"

"Yeah, I'm sure. I put them in the little cubbyhole last night, just like you told me to, but they weren't there when I checked this morning. They're gone. Somebody stole them, all right."

"Oh my goodness. That's terrible," he stammered. "Nothing like this has ever happened on my car," he said defensively and quickly stepped over to my doorway. He reached up to a little door on the wall outside of my roomette, the same door I had checked when I heard the noise. Click. That was it, the sound I had heard in the middle of the night. He opened the door and I could see the look of relief on his face. He turned and smiled at me, then he reached in and pulled out my shoes. "Are these yours, sir?" he asked and gave me a look that sort of said "what kind of dummy are you, anyway?"

"They're just like I left them. They're all polished up. Nice and shiny, just like new."

"Where'd they come from?"

"Right out of the little compartment," he answered happily.

"But they weren't there when I checked this morning," I replied. "The compartment was empty."

"You must have checked when I had your shoes out polishing them," smiled the porter.

"Yeah, sure," I mumbled and looked down, checking his feet. There was no fear of him keeping my shoes. He would never get his size twelves into my size nines.

"You enjoy your breakfast, sir, while I make up your quarters and make sure that no one else's shoes were stolen."

"Right."

As I walked toward the dining car, my feet nestled in my oxfords, I didn't even notice the snug-fitting shoes rubbing on my blisters.

THE EMERGENCY CORD

There had been several porters on the train as my journey toward the Rockcliffe training centre moved across the prairies and Northern Ontario. The latest porter who was now with us, somewhere in Northern Ontario, had for some reason taken a real liking to the kid from the stump farm. At every possible opportunity he stopped and talked and flashed his big friendly smile. He was a fountain of knowledge and spewed forth more information about the region than it was possible to absorb. One tidbit that did not go unnoticed, however, was the fact that in Ontario, we were old enough to purchase a bottle of grog at a provincial grog shop. Armed with this information, my travelling companions and I pooled our resources and we waited, not so patiently, for the next stop. We could be thankful that our train was being pulled by an old steam engine, for they needed regular servicing stops to take on coal and water. We needed a town where the train would have to stop to take on these necessities and while the train was being serviced, a speedy prairie boy would have enough time to make the mercy run.

Finally, in this frozen northland, in an unknown town in the heavily forested, snow-covered countryside, the train pulled into a station and the train crew began the task of servicing the train. The train had barely stopped when our designated man, not me for I was not seen as being very speedy, bailed out of the train. The porter had to hurry to set his little stool on the platform and get his fingers out of the way or run the risk of having them trampled by the speedy runner. As the maintenance crew swarmed over the train, the dash for grog was on.

The runner paused long enough to ask a quick question, which direction, of one of the hustling trainmen. A finger pointed south to a street, a flick of the trainman's wrist as he indicated a turn back to the east, then our man bolted away. Two of us stood at the open gate on our car and watched as our man raced away from the station, toward, we presumed, the town centre. At previous service stops along the way, the service crews seemed to take forever. But here, in frozen snow-covered northern Ontario, the crew seemed to be working at double time. I watched the man with his little steel hammer walk the length of the train and tap each steel wheel. Even the wheel tapper, who in other towns seemed to crawl along the train at a snail's pace, was suddenly in a hurry. Ping, ping, ping rang the hammer. Trainmen were scurrying in every direction and time flew as we watched and waited for our troop mate to return. It seemed impossible, it had to have been longer, but in only a matter of seconds the train was serviced.

From somewhere on the platform the conductor called out, "All aboard".

The friendly porter, waiting for the call, picked up his

little foot stool and stepped onto the train. He leaned out for a last look around, then climbed on board. He closed the gate, flashed his friendly smile and joked for a second, then turned to walk into the car. The steam engine huffed and puffed, metal moaned and creaked in the frigid weather and slowly the train started to chug. Horror upon horror, we were moving forward, out of this little town without our buddy. Then the whistle blew. It was an eerie mournful wail. It seemed to say 'so long' to our new friend. Maybe he wasn't as speedy as we thought.

"Hey, we can't leave yet. Our partner's not back," I shouted at the porter. "You'll have to stop the train."

"I don't think I can do that," he smiled. "Once the engineer gets this baby moving, the only way to stop it is to pull the emergency cord."

"What's that?" I asked. I had heard of an emergency brake, but never an emergency cord on a train.

"There," he said and pointed to a cord running overhead. "That there is an emergency cord."

"That little cord? That's gonna stop this train?" I asked.

"Yes sir," he replied. "That little cord right there. If somebody were to pull that little cord, this train stops." He chuckled and walked into the car.

I leaned out of the car, over the gate, frantically searching the lonely street. Except for the train crew, who were now moving at a snail's pace, the street was vacant. There was not even a glimpse of a rapidly moving person.

I looked up at the emergency cord. Boy, I thought, everybody tries to have fun with us country boys. Did he really believe that I was gullible enough to think that little cord would stop this train? Who did he think he was talking to, I wondered? I glanced at my partner as I reached up and very tentatively touched the cord. Just as I thought, nothing happened. The engine was chugging faster and the train continued to pick up speed. I looked back at the empty street. I looked at my partner again. I returned my attention to the cord. Now, I knew that it would be wrong to just reach up and pull that cord, because it was for an emergency. But since one of our boys wasn't back yet, I figured this was an emergency. Slowly I reached up again and gave the cord a gentle tug. Well, maybe it was more then a gentle tug, for suddenly, a strange thing happened. Without any warning, I was thrown forward. My lips led the way and stuck fast, right smack dab onto the end of the car. The great train jerked, the couplings clanged and the steel wheels squealed loudly as metal skidded on metal and the whole train came to a sudden grinding halt.

My friend and I peeled ourselves off the end of the car as the area became a beehive of activity. Instantly, conductors, porters and trainmen were running to and fro. I was checking my lip to see if there was any blood as our porter came racing out of the car. He flung open the gate and threw his little footstool on the platform.

"What happened?" I asked the friendly man as he hurried about his duties.

"The train's stopped," he puffed. "Somethin's wrong with the train," he puffed and hurried off down the platform.

On the platform, he joined the melee of train personnel as they ran first one way, then the other. They searched under the cars, between the cars and even in the cars as they sought the source of the trouble. The man with the hammer walked by again. Ping, ping, ping came the sound of the hammer as he walked along rapping each wheel. After several minutes and lots of head-shaking and arm-waving, the train was obviously deemed to be Railworthy.

"All aboard," called the conductor for the second time.

Again our porter threw his little foot stool onto the train and slammed the gate shut.

"What does that mean? What happened?" I asked.

This time there was no friendly smile, no flashing of teeth, only a scowl as he stared at us, then at the emergency cord. "It usually means that we have a problem on the train, and we can't leave the station until we check it out," he replied.

"Man, that train sure stopped in a hurry," I stated, touching a tender spot where I had unintentionally kissed the back wall. "I think I'm getting a fat lip from hitting the car."

"People get more then a fat lip from something like this," snapped our porter. He did not sound nearly as happy and friendly as he had been. He appeared to be just a bit annoyed as he cast us a not-so-friendly glance before turning and stomping past us into his car. Once more the whistle blew, the metal moaned and creaked and the train chugged, building a head of steam.

My partner and I stood fast at our post. We scanned the street diligently, searching for any sign of our lost buddy. It appeared that he had either deserted or become lost in the bowels of this frozen little metropolis. Then, in the distance I saw him. Our long-lost buddy appeared on the street. His legs were pumping like pistons as he raced for the station and the departing train. I was very happy to see him racing down the road clutching a bag of goodies. Oh, he was fast all right. We had made a good choice, I thought, as he sped toward the station. But he was too far away. He was not going to make it. It would be a shame for him to have gone through all that trouble and then be left standing at the station.

From where I stood, nothing had changed. Our man on a mission had not returned, the train was once more leaving the station and our emergency still existed. I looked both ways, then again at my partner. He gave me the nod. Once more my eyes were drawn to the cord. Slowly, tentatively I reached upwards. "Brace yourself," I mentioned to my partner as my fingers wrapped around the cord.

The wheels again screeched as the train ground to a halt.

"Now what's the problem?" I asked the porter, who was beginning to break a sweat as he bolted through the door.

"Some idiot keeps pulling the emergency cord," he snorted as he threw open the gate and flung his little foot stool onto the platform. "If this keeps up, we're going to be late, we'll be way off schedule."

It appeared to me, a non-railroader and a novice in these matters, that the second unscheduled delay was being viewed as a far more serious matter. This time, in the midst of confusion, I watched the wheel tapper making his rounds. He was taking more interest in his job. He stopped at each wheel and eyeballed it critically before he gave it an extra hard tap. Ping. Metal rang off metal as he tapped the wheel, then he stayed and listened to the ringing sound die in the frozen air before proceeding to the next. Pinnnggg he tapped the next wheel and the next as he walked, eyeballed, rapped, waited, then walked again. To me it looked like he was the only man who was not in a state of panic.

Railroaders had a language all their own for dealing with unscheduled events or a persistent problem that appeared to have no easy solutions. Being a country boy myself, the combination of cursing, hollering, head-shaking, arm-waving and even some kicking at imaginary objects did not make much sense. But I'm sure that to seasoned wily veterans of the railroad each movement, every word, had a purpose. While chaos reigned supreme, another miracle occurred. A speeding body raced off the street onto the platform. He fit right in with the bustling crew. Without being detected and well before the search was completed, our lost buddy worked his way through the confusion and bounded into our car. Completely spent from his harrowing ordeal, he collapsed on the floor.

"Man, what took you so long?" asked my other troop mate. "Did you have to bottle the stuff yourself?"

"That guy tells us we can buy booze," he puffed. "What he didn't tell us was that you can only buy booze if you have a permit," he grumbled and slumped against the car gasping for breath.

"Hey, you did us proud, man, not only did you get a permit, but you got the goodies," I noted and tapped the brown paper bag.

"No, I didn't get a permit. That's what took me so long," he mumbled through gasps. "I musta begged a dozen guys before I found an old boy who would let me use his." After he caught his breath, he looked up. "I can tell you guys, when I heard that train whistle, I thought for sure I was gonna miss the train. Boy, am I ever glad it takes these guys forever to service a train. You guys ever notice how long it takes?"

"Oh, I think we have a pretty good idea," chuckled my partner. "C'mon guys, let's go to my room and have a drink to celebrate."

"Celebrate what?" asked the runner.

"Your safe return," he replied.

Just then, a frazzled looking porter threw his little step stool into the car and slowly climbed aboard. We watched while he dropped the floor piece and closed the gate. He followed us into the car and zigzagged along behind us to the roomettes. "You look like you could use some refreshments," I commented. "Would you like to join us in a little toast to our friend here, the fastest man in Northern Ontario?"

"I don't think I want to join you boys for nothin'," he snorted. "Right now, I just wish you was on somebody else's car." I noted that we were no longer gentlemen; at this last stop we had reverted to 'boys'.

"Maybe a little later, then?" I suggested. "You know, you're welcome to join us anytime."

"Maybe never," he snorted. "I hope that stuff was worth the effort. In fact, I hope you boys choke on it."

"And a jolly good day to you, too," I chuckled. "By the way, what time do we get into Ottawa?" I asked.

"Not soon enough," he replied. "We was supposed to be there late tomorrow afternoon, but at the rate we're going we may never get there."

There was lots of time to celebrate our buddy's successful dash in the frozen north. In the not-so-comfortable cramped quarters, with two of us crammed into the armchair and one man sitting on the john, we drank a toast. We toasted the train ride. We toasted the mad dash across the frozen north. We toasted each other. We toasted everything we could think of. In the waning hours, when the contents of the bottle had been extracted, the toasts had ceased and we three were wiser than a whole tree full of owls. It was time to turn in. It would be good to get some shut-eye before reporting for duty.

But sleep was not in the cards. Early, very early in the morning, when it seemed my head had just barely hit the pillow, the face of a very happy porter poked through the curtain door in my roomette. He had unzipped it, or I had forgotten to zip it up, and he was grinning from ear to ear. "Git yourself up and outta my car," he warbled cheerfully. "We're in Ottawa."

"What do you mean we're in Ottawa?" I mumbled. "We

can't be! We just went to bed." I looked out the window. The shade was still up but the sun wasn't. "Look. It's still dark outside. I thought you told us that we're not supposed to get into Ottawa until later this afternoon," I moaned.

"Oh, did I say that?" he smiled. "Well, I meant to say tonight, later tonight or early in the morning. I am sorry, you know I'm not really sure what I meant to say, but I guess I must have made a mistake. You know, sometimes after a stressful ordeal, I make mistakes," he chuckled. "Now, you better get moving, 'cause I want you off my car, and the sooner the better." I could hear him laughing and whistling all the way down the corridor.

I was a very groggy young man when I emerged from my roomette to face the day. Ottawa had arrived about twelve hours earlier then expected. The smiling porter flashed an extra big toothy smile as I groped for the handrail and almost took a nosedive off his stool.

We were greeted at the station by an equally sleepy-looking member from the training centre at Rockcliffe. He did not appear all that happy that he had drawn the short straw this early in the morning. He wasted little time and few words as he hustled us into the waiting patrol car and whisked us though the streets of the nation's capital. It was a sight that I had really been looking forward to, but it, like the night, drifted past me. I'd have to return and see what I missed. Man, I hoped that there was at least one bed in Rockcliffe with my name on it. But I was soon to learn that there was no rest for the weary. Folks at Rockcliffe were not as happy to see us as I had thought. I was shown a bed, a welcome sight, and told that it was mine. I was about to park my aching carcass on it, but before that happened I was hustled out of the room and shown the mess hall. Here I was at least allowed to sit, but lo and behold, I sat at the wrong table. That table belonged to one of the senior troops and senior troop members did not lower themselves to mix with scruff like myself. In no uncertain words I was told to get something to eat and park my useless body somewhere else to eat it, then if I knew what was good for me, I'd report outside the front of the barracks for duty.

For some unknown reason, the breakfast did not look very appetizing. But I took my tray and plunked my butt down at the closest table. That was another mistake, for that table too was reserved for persons senior and far superior to me. One thing became very clear and obvious in a hurry. Folks around the training centre wasted precious little time in kicking my butt about. Obviously, I was a slow learner for this time I was directed to a vacant table at the rear of the room.

After a quick breakfast, which I could not eat, I dragged myself out to the front of the barracks. When called on to fall in, I didn't really need any prompting. I could have gladly fallen in all right, face first in the snow would have been welcome at that moment. But laying down was not in the cards. I along with others was issued a shovel and assigned a section of sidewalk to clear. I was out near the back of the barracks block surveying my surroundings. I was not a well man. I was tired, my stomach kept sending me mixed messages, and I had something that felt like a knife blade running right through one eye into the back of my head. The knife was giving me a terrible headache. Every movement was torture.

Through hazy, bleary eyes, I observed the grounds of the Rockcliffe training base. The first thing I noticed was the snow. There was tons of snow, about two feet of it covered the grounds. There were trees, maple or oak? I had no idea, but I knew we didn't have anything like them on the stump farm. They were huge trees with massive limbs spreading their leafless tentacles far and wide. Trees appeared to cover all the grounds that were not taken up by buildings, and there were a lot of buildings. The barracks block, my new home, housed the recruits, the mess hall, the rec area and the gym.

Behind the barracks block was a small building, the Administration Centre. Across the street were the riding stables and next to them, right beside the front gate, a little museum. To the south of the barracks block were a number of smaller buildings, lecture halls, pistol range (in the basement of one of the lecture halls) and residences including that of the Commissioner of the force. To the north, beyond a grove of trees, were the garage and a huge parking lot. To the west lay a huge open field that was at the end of the runway at the Rockcliffe Air Force base. Beyond the field was the Ottawa river.

My troop would not be squadded until all thirty-two of us arrived. In the meantime, I along with a few of my future troop mates who had also arrived early at Rockcliffe had been assigned a shovel. Once in camp, squadded or not, everyone worked. Our task for this day was snow removal.

I really felt ill when I thought that I would probably have to shovel all the sidewalks that connected these buildings. Right then, I knew I needed all the help I could get if I was going to make it through this day, so I was leaning quite heavily on the only means of support, the issue shovel, to help me prepare for this onerous day. A movement over by the stables caught my eye. I stopped the heavy leaning long enough to lift my head and watch in awe as the cloud of steam that had burst forth from the stables moved along the sidewalk. It was followed closely by an escort, two officers.

They were, I concluded, probably recruits, dressed in their brown uniforms (fatigues they called them) and they marched smartly along, about two steps behind the cloud. Steam billowed forth into the frosty afternoon air as the misty form, a man, moved rapidly along the sidewalk. Out to the roadway in front of the administration building they came. They executed a smart right turn at the roadway and the cloud drifted ahead of them, marching west to a 'T' intersection. There they performed an equally smart left turn and marched toward the front of the barracks.

"What do you make of that?" I asked one of the other recruits who I noticed was working his shovel at the same angle I was.

"Beats me," he replied, shaking his head. "I never saw nothing like that before in my life."

"Sorta looked like a guy in a cloud of steam, didn't it?"

"That's sure enough what it looked like," he agreed.

"You think he might be some kind of misty man?" I chuckled.

"You there. Get back to work. That's enough goofing off for one day, unless of course you'd like a taste of the same medicine?" snarled a constable who had suddenly appeared out of nowhere and his sharp tone snapped me back to reality and the task at hand. He was in charge of our little work detail. This important person was no longer a recruit, but a real live, honest-to-goodness member of the force. He had graduated some time earlier and was assigned to mother green recruits. He did not appear to me to be happy with his lot in life.

"And what medicine would that be?" I foolishly asked, rotating slowly on the end of my shovel to face him. Turning my head hurt too much.

"You...you stand at attention when you address me, you horrible excuse for a human being," he growled and strode rapidly toward me. There was absolutely no doubt whatsoever in his mind about who was the superior being in this confrontation and he was going to make sure that there was no doubt in mine, either.

My earlier army cadet training put me in real good stead and I figured most likely right at the head of the class. I was fortunate enough to know what he meant by standing at attention. I immediately straightened up, I clicked my heels together, I tucked my shovel neatly under my right arm, sorta like it was a rifle. The sudden movement sent another shockwave knifing through my other eye, where it ricocheted around the back of my skull. However, I bit my tongue and I stood bolt upright staring straight ahead. There, I winced, this is one 'horrible excuse for a human being' that knows what he's doing. I would have smiled, but even my lips hurt. Somehow, I was standing at attention, and if my shovel had been a rifle, I would have ordered arms. Through the pain, I couldn't hide a feeling of smugness that I had 'ordered shovels' instead and without even being told.

From the corner of my eye, I could see my new-found troop mates rapidly shovelling. They resembled a whole passel of side hill gougers. Man, they had snow flying in every direction as they worked to avoid the same fate, whatever that might be, that awaited me.

"In the future, when you talk to me, you will also acknowledge my rank," stormed the very irritated constable. He had arrived in front of me and his nose was only inches from mine. "The question will be 'What medicine would that be, constable?' Do you understand me, you horrible little man?" he bellowed and stood in my face, glaring into my eyes.

73

"Yes, that's clear," I shouted back to insure that he heard me. Now, I might be a 'horrible little man', but even I, 'a horrible little man', could follow instructions to a 'T'.

Suddenly, he stopped and stared at me. His jaw dropped and he seemed to have trouble finding the right words. "Is...is there something wrong with your eyes, man?" he asked, moving in for a real good close-up of my eyes. Then he recoiled as if he had just looked into the eyes of death. There was no doubt from his sudden reaction and the sound of his voice that he was more than a little concerned. "Your eyes, man...they look like...." he started to lean forward for another look and then stepped back smartly lest he, too, be smitten with the same affliction. "Man, your eyes, they look terrible, sick, they're all bloodshot. You got pinkeye or somethin'?"

"Oh no, they're fine," I replied, trying to make light of the situation. "It's nothing that a little sleep won't cure. You see, we had a late night on the train and...."

"Didn't I make myself clear? You...you poor excuse for a human being? When you address me, it's 'Yes, that's clear constable'," he barked, obviously having forgotten his concern for my eyes. The veins on his neck were sticking out like garden hoses.

I could feel the spray and gobs of spit that spewed forth freezing on my face. Man, my stock was fading fast, how low could it get, I wondered? Now I had been reduced to a poor excuse for a human being. I made up my mind to try to improve on that rating and I answered back in a loud voice that sent stabbing pains through my head and could best be described as a healthy yell. "Yes, that's clear, constable."

"Now, that's better," he sneered at me, safe in the knowledge that finally we were on the same playing field. I now knew he was a constable. A man of rank, albeit quite small, and authority. He turned and strutted away, not bothering to answer my question. "Give me ten and then follow me. I have another assignment for smart-asses like you," he warbled triumphantly into the winter air.

"Give you ten what...constable?" I asked.

"Pushups," he bellowed for all to hear. "Don't you know anything? Give me ten pushups."

Ten pushups later, with my shovel tucked neatly under my arm, I marched along behind the constable. Snow was still flying from the shovels at the back of the barracks block as we marched around to the front of the barracks. Past the front doors we marched, past the barracks and along the treed roadway. We turned right onto a small trail that led to a huge open field. We marched down a small hill that ran back in front of the barracks block. At the bottom of the hill we stopped and we both stared out across the field of snow to a line of trees that marked the Ottawa River. A portion of the small field to the right of the path looked like a herd of cows had been milling about in the deep snow. There were lots of footprints, footprints that had taken giant strides leading out in every direction. It almost looked like spokes leading from the hub of a wheel. Some folks had left this place in one big hurry, I thought.

"Okay constable, we'll see just how smart you really are," he laughed. It was a sinister laugh as he added, "You can start shovelling, anytime."

"Here, constable?" I asked, looking at the enormous snow-covered field that was flatter then a griddle. Did he really think that I, this horrible excuse for a human being, could shovel all this snow? "But, why would anyone shovel here?"

"Because this here is the parade square, it is where we march, but first it needs to be shovelled off. However, the main reason I want you down here is that, out here in this field, there are no distractions for your pea-sized brain. And because there's no one out here for you to talk to, all you have to do is shovel. Now get busy, and I don't want to hear another word from you."

I had to admit, this wasn't really the field I had in mind when I said I wanted to do field work when I left Alberta. I could only thank my lucky stars that the old ranger wasn't around to see me. However, I had a feeling he would have agreed that it was the perfect job for a young fella with a pea-sized brain. The constable watched me carefully as I bent over to take the scoop of snow. I lifted the first shovelful and could not stifle the moan. Man, everything hurt me on this field trip. I scooped several shovels of snow, and sure enough, down about two feet, under all the snow, I did indeed find a paved surface. I looked at the depth of the snow and the size of the field. I suddenly had this sinking feeling that this could well be the field where I was going to be for the rest of the winter. I didn't figure I needed much more than the pea-sized brain I possessed to handle the task I had been assigned. I had this terrible feeling that my six shooter and my shiny new cruiser could very easily be given to someone with a greater cranial capacity than I.

Satisfied that the shovel was now being used for the purpose it was intended, my overseer turned and marched triumphantly away. He had not yet marched up the small hill when I came across a familiar object imbedded in the snow. It appeared to be a rather large cartridge of some kind. Now, I had long been a collector of cartridges, and knew many by sight, but this particular one was new to me. I had never seen one like it. From its snowy resting place, I could hear it call to me, demanding that I pick it up and give it a good close look-see. But first, my pea-sized brain told me that I had better check to see that all was clear before I made another blunder. I surveyed the area carefully. The constable was now marching up the hill, his back turned to me. All was clear.

Slowly, I bent down and lifted the cartridge from its bed of snow. It had been warm when it was discarded and clumps of ice and snow clung to its smooth surface. I vigorously brushed it clean with my gloves, then held it up to be admired. It was larger than any cartridges that I had, but unfortunately it was spent and of no use to me. The cartridges in my collection were all live, so I tossed it to one side and continued to shovel.

Now, even in cold weather, a man can work up a sweat and a man suffering as I was can really sweat. Sweating rather profusely, after tossing just a few shovels of snow, I instinctively wiped my brow with my mitts. In an instant, my eyes began to water and burn like crazy. The stabbing pains were now like bolts of lightning shooting through my head. My first attempt at field work was not going well at all, in fact my whole world was rapidly coming unglued. Everything, the snowy field, the trees, the barracks, was no longer clear. They weren't even blurry, they were disappearing as the light of day suddenly turned to dark. "I'm going blind," I shouted. I dropped my shovel and with huge giant strides deserted my field. Through the fading light that was left in my burned-out eyeballs, I charged through the snow heading for the hill, the trail, the road and hopefully the barracks. I knew I had to get to the barracks. I stumbled up the hill, onto the path to the road. I blew past the constable who wisely stepped aside. It would not look good on his record to be run down by a blind poor excuse for a human being, with a pea-sized brain. By the time I reached the barracks my eyes were watering and burning so bad that I could hardly see a thing. I stumbled through the front doors, searching to find the washrooms, then the sinks. There, with a tap running full blast I worked vigorously to put out the fire. I had my head right down under the tap, splashing cold water in my eyes.

Over the sound of the water blasting into the sink and my frantic splashing came a familiar sound. "You, you...you horrible little man, you left your post without permission," I heard the constable scream at me.

"I'm going blind, you idiot," I screamed back. "Can't you see, I'm going blind? I can't see nothing."

"I'm going blind, you idiot. Can't you see, I'm going blind? I can't see nothing, CONSTABLE," he roared, repeating every word. "Can't you remember anything? I just finished telling you that you will address me by my rank at all times."

Man, I thought, what a day this has been. I'm going blind and all this idiot is worried about is me calling him constable. "I'm sorry, constable," I burbled through the water. "But I'm going blind. Everything's blurry and I can't see anything...constable."

After what seemed to be an eternity things started to get a little better. There was only the sound of running water when I raised my head. The burning had lessened, but was not entirely gone and my eyes were still watering like crazy. The sharp pains darting in and out of the back of my head persisted. Images were once again coming into focus. I looked around the room and was relieved to see that the detail was returning. Then I saw him. He was standing by himself, my overseer was just inside the door, standing with his legs apart and his hands behind his back. He rocked back and forth on his heels while he waited. It was comforting to know that he was there to make sure that I was okay. I felt better knowing that for all the bluster, he really cared.

"Congratulations, you imbecile," he finally sneered and shook the confidence I had just imagined. "It looks like you just found the tear gas canister we fired a couple of weeks ago. Do you feel a little better now, you poor boy?"

So that explained those tracks on the field. Others had probably received a good dose of what I rubbed in my eyes. No wonder they took off out of there like scared rabbits. "Well, I don't mind telling you, constable, I was scared. I thought for sure I was going blind, constable," I mumbled. I tried to stare at him through teary eyes, but my eyelids kept flapping like shutters in a windstorm.

"You'll be all right," he snarled. "Now give me ten for failing to call me constable and twenty for leaving your post without permission."

"You gotta be kidding...constable," I questioned him, remembering at the last second to address him properly.

"I don't kid," he snapped. He stood there and waited until I had finished the thirty pushups. "Now get back to your post and don't leave until I tell you to," he ordered as I struggled to my feet.

Thirty pushups later I was back on the parade square, back on the snow-covered field. I took a minute to look west. Somewhere out across that field and river was Western Canada...Alberta...Edson and home. What had I done to myself, I wondered as I reflected on my first day in training. And what a first day it had been. I learned more about myself in a day than I had learned in twenty years, and none of it was good. Because of the eye thing, I knew for certain that illness would not get me any sympathy or excuse me from any duty. I now knew that everybody in Rockcliffe had a rank, even if it was only constable and I for one would be addressing them properly, according to their rank. In future I would not be picking up any item that was lying around loose and otherwise unattached. But after all, I smiled, I had been outside all day on my first field trip in the RCMP. Now, I had to ask myself, had this been a field trip, or had this been a field trip?

THE MISTY MAN

One activity, I learned quickly, was the same for recruits, squadded or not, senior or junior. It was a daily task that we could all look forward to: the cleaning of the stables. Every day, seven days a week, fifty-two weeks a year, bright and early in the morning, recruits were assembled in front of the barracks and marched to the stables. There they would shovel and sweep up horse shit, wash and groom horses, pitch straw and hay and feed each horse a little oats. At the end of the drill they would march back to the barracks.

Now, many people may think that shoveling horse shit is a very simple straightforward task. But I am here to tell you that is not so. Like all good training programs, there is a reason for every activity. And even dunging out the barn has to be done according to specific criteria. Failure to comply is a very serious matter and highly frowned upon. Those bold or silly enough to breach the accepted rule would inevitably suffer the consequences. Very negative consequences, as I was about to find out.

My troop, the junior troop in training, 'rabble' to just about everybody we came in contact with, had not yet come into existence. A full compliment of 32 men was required before the troop would be squadded. On the day in question, those of us who had arrived early in camp, a loose collection of 'rabble', had been marched over to the barns with one of the senior troops. We had been tacked on to the end of the troop and yes, we probably looked like 'rabble' as we trundled along, each of us marching to our own drummer.

The routine had been unfolding the same as any other day, the horse shit and straw had been shoveled, swept and removed from the stalls and the gutters. I had picked up a sponge and a bucket of warm water to wash a horse. Since my troop had not yet been squadded, I had not been assigned a horse and like the rest of the 'rabble' I consorted with, I was pushed towards a different horse every morning. Yes, I was going to be washing a horse and today the lucky horse was a male. Previously, I had been shoved into stalls with mares whose eyes, noses and butts I had washed with the sponge and warm water. The mares had always stood quietly and accepted their cleansing graciously.

This horse was a little different and for some reason seemed to be a little more anxious. In fact, I could have sworn that old gelding was smiling at me as I carefully sponged out his eyes and his nose. When I finished washing the necessary head parts, I turned and walked towards his rear end. I noticed that his tail was already high in the air as he anticipated the warm water and sponge. Then he started to do a little two-step. Instinctively I stepped back to avoid the hooves and assess the situation. I was somewhat taken aback at what hung before me. "Oh no," I protested when I saw what else he had exposed. "There's no way I'm gonna wash that thing off." I stepped to the rear of the stall and thrust the sponge under his raised tail. Warm water splashed onto his butt, then I turned and walked out of the stall. The horse was furious and indignant and he threw a fit. He snorted and stomped like a spoiled kid protesting the omission.

'What's the matter with that horse?" barked the instructor who came running down the length of the stable.

"I have no idea, corporal," I replied.

"Did you wash him down properly?"

"Every inch of him, corporal," I lied.

"Did you use cold water, man?" he asked and thrust his hand into the bucket.

"No, corporal," I replied. He entered the stall and checked the horse from nose to tail. Both he and the horse eyed me suspiciously.

After the horses had been groomed and fed hay as well as their portion of oats, the floors were swept clean. Some of the 'rabble' had been handed brooms, and they had horse shit, straw and dust flying in every direction. One of the 'rabble' would be pushing refuse into the broom of the next, as they wielded the heavy brooms this way and that. There was a lot of grunting, groaning and cursing accompanying the attempt to clean the place and push the mess to the back of the stables. The effort could be best described as a rearranging of the contents on the floor.

It was the senior troop who completed the job. It was something to see the well trained seasoned veteran recruits from the senior troop sweep the stables. With push brooms, they lined up shoulder to shoulder across the width of the stables and working in unison, like a well-oiled machine, they moved from one end of the stables to the other. Each broom was lifted, pulled back, snapped on the floor and pushed forward at the same time. Each man in the line was like an extension of the other as the brooms snapped, then scraped across the floor. A piece of 'rabble' like myself had to be careful not to get in the way of such efficiency lest you end up in the manure bin.

The team had brushed the stable floor clean from one end to the other. I thought every task had been performed and the stables looked the same as they had every other morning. The floors couldn't have been any cleaner if they had been spit-polished.

The group was then marshaled in front of the water troughs, horse troughs, waiting for the man in charge to complete his inspection, an inspection that would confirm every detail had been properly attended to. I along with everyone else waited impatiently for the word so that we could be marched back to the barracks and breakfast. Up to this point, except for the frustrated gelding, the routine appeared to have been the same as every other morning, but for some reason, there was not the customary "Good job, lads". Apparently, the man had detected a problem and it concerned him greatly. Suddenly, he exploded. He was, to say the least, visibly upset. Stomping about like a madman in front of the troop, he began to vent his spleen.

"If there's one thing I cannot tolerate, will not tolerate, it's a sloppy, slovenly, poor excuse for a man," he ranted as he paced back and forth in front of the troop. We all stood stiffly at attention, staring straight ahead. I, personally, was dying to have a look around and see who among us had been singled out as the misfit. Who was this sloppy, slovenly, poor excuse for a man who was delaying us from returning to the barracks and breakfast? Did he not know that there was precious little time to march back, get showered, get changed, eat breakfast, clean up the room for inspection and fall in at the front of the barracks? What was it that this sloppy, slovenly, poor excuse for a man had done, or forgotten to do? Had he not recognized the rank of the instructor? My curiosity was killing me, but like everyone else, I stood frozen in my boots, afraid to move a muscle, even an eye muscle. Instructors had a reputation for being keenly observant. They were eagle-eyed and were notoriously adept at detecting the slightest movement in the ranks.

"You call yourselves 'the cream of the crop', 'Canada's finest'....Well, I can tell you what you really are. You're the cream of the crop, all right, 'the sour cream'. You're Canada's nothing. Nothing, I tell you! There now, how do you like them apples, eh? 'Sour cream', that's what I call you and that's what you are!" he bellowed. I couldn't see him, but I could hear him and I could feel those fiery eyes, feel them burning a hole right through every man assembled before the horse troughs as he stormed along the ranks.

"You...you horrible excuse for a human being," he snarled at someone to my left. "One step forward. Queek Marhhh." Recognizing my calling from a previous encounter, I knew I fit the last description and was about to step forward and receive my just reward when from the corner of my eye, I saw movement. I breathed a sigh of relief as this day's horrible excuse for a human being stepped forward. One hesitant step before tentatively coming to a halt. Man, I thought, now there were two us, two horrible excuses for human beings in the same troop and lucky for me, for I had just dodged a bullet.

"This...this horrible little man has failed to properly care for his horse this morning," roared the incensed instructor as he strutted back and forth along the length of the troop. So furious was he that he was waving his riding crop over his head, swatting at some imaginary object. "In this man's force, that is an unpardonable sin, gentlemen. A man who does not care for his horse, does not care for himself. And anyone who does not care for himself does not care for his troop. Would you gentlemen want to trust your lives to someone who does not care for himself? I don't think so. I know I wouldn't. I want someone I can depend on, someone I can trust. This horrible excuse for a human being does not deserve to be in the presence of real men. He is a disgrace, to you, to me, to the force. He does not deserve your loyalty. Do you agree with me, gentlemen?" he asked.

No one answered following the question. I was too busy thanking the gods that I had been spared and trying to figure out what heinous crime had been committed to warrant such an outburst. Had the horse's eyes not been washed out, had his nose not been wiped, or maybe his arse hadn't been sponged off properly. If so, how had the instructor known? Who had told him? Had it been the horse? You know, the more I thought about it, the more convinced I became that those ruddy horses seemed to be almost human. I had just about convinced myself that it was the horse, that one of them could probably talk, when I was rudely jarred back to the present.

"Gentlemen, I asked you a question," roared the instructor. "Now, I think that I deserve an answer. For my benefit, all together now, do you agree with me, gentlemen?"

Even to a green recruit like me, another horrible little man, the answer was obvious. "Yes corporal," came the unified response. Taking a peek out of the corner of my eye, I noticed that the horrible excuse for a human being standing one step in front of the troop was shivering like a leaf in the wind. With a build-up like this he'll get fifty push-ups, I thought to myself.

"Very good gentlemen, I am impressed with your wisdom," he cooed. "Now, when a man screws up, there must be some consequences for his actions. And gentlemen, I am here to tell you that there are. Do I make myself clear, gentlemen?" he asked and slapped his riding crop into the palm of his hand. Thwack. Thwack. Thwack. The sound reverberated throughout the stables.

"Very clear, corporal," came the response.

"Gentlemen," he spoke loud and clear. "I have to go into the tack room for about five minutes. I want you to understand that I'll be leaving you here, alone, with this horrible excuse for a human being, for a full five minutes. I know you'll do the right thing." Then he walked over to the horse trough and looked down into the ice cold clear water and tapped his riding crop on the edge of the trough. The guilty had been found, there was no trial, but the penalty had been decided. With that, the instructor turned and marched away, triumphantly.

Before I knew what was happening, there was a flurry of activity. Leather soles scraped and stomped on the concrete floor and I was almost trampled by the senior troop as they raced past me. I stood perfectly still and watched in amazement as the other horrible excuse for a human being, who only a moment earlier had been standing one pace in front, shivering and shaking, was swept off his feet. Strong arms grabbed him, clasping his arms, legs and torso tightly, and hoisted his writhing body into the air. Across the concrete floor they moved, and wrestled him to the edge of the horse-trough.

"What in the hell did I do?" he wailed. "C'mon fellas, I didn't do nothing. Hel...." The horrible excuse for a human being started to yell, but the sound of his voice was drowned out as he was plunged into the water.

I was totally amazed at what was happening and realized that I was still standing at attention. I left my post and quietly slipped over to the horse-trough. Through the water, at the bottom of the trough, I could see this pair of deep blue eyes staring up at me. They were wide open, scared, and pleading. Man, was that one scared lot of sour cream. No, petrified lot of sour cream would be a better description. I had seen fear, but never before had I seen a pair of blue eyes with so much fear in them.

"You're drowning him," I shouted at the big guy who had both hands submerged in the water. One hand was on the neck, the other on the chest. He was doing more then his share of holding him down.

"Bugger off, puke," growled the big guy who suddenly seemed much bigger when he shot me the dirtiest look out of a pair of evil steely blue eyes.

"Run," my brain yelled at my legs. "Run, you fool, or you're next." But when I looked back into the trough and the deep blue eyes, I was frozen. I couldn't move. "But, but you're drowning him," I protested.

"I said bugger off, before you get some of the same medicine," he growled again.

"But, he's drowning," I replied. "Look, there's bubbles coming out of his mouth." At the bottom of the trough, the blue eyes shimmered as the bubbles flashed in front of them. The eyes were doing the dance of fear when the last bubbles stopped and wobbled to the top of the horse trough. It was then that the same strong arms hauled his head out of the water. The poor, horrible excuse for a human being was left sitting in the trough, in the icy water. He sat there sputtering and gasping for air. He finally mustered enough strength to crawl over the side of the trough and fell to the floor along with several gallons of ice cold water. Other members of the senior troop had rushed to get push brooms and they hurriedly swept up the water and almost the horrible excuse for a human being, who was groveling around on the floor. He struggled to get out of the way of the sweepers and back to his place in the ranks.

"Thanks to this puke, I'm probably gonna miss my breakfast now," growled the big guy with the steely-blue eyes.

"I wish they'd stop accepting this sort of scum," chimed in another. "The only thing you get out of guys like this is a lot of misery and more hard work."

"Well, this oughta teach them all a lesson they won't soon forget," laughed the first guy.

The troop was back in formation, including a very cold and wet horrible excuse for a human being, when the instructor returned. Without so much as a glance at the wet floor or another word on the crime or its consequence, he marched us out of the stable.

As I marched along, I noticed that the sour cream in front of me looked very much like a drowned rat. We were both in our proper places, two horrible excuses for human beings trailing along at the end of the senior troop. The drowned rat transformed as we marched through the doors into the winter morning. As the blast of cold air hit him, he was instantly transformed into a cloud of steam.

I was the escort now, as I marched along behind the misty man.

FIT FOR A SADDLE

Unless a recruit was unlucky enough to draw extra duties, Saturdays and Sundays at the training centre were normally times to recharge the batteries. This particular Saturday started out to be the same as many others. I did my laundry, blued my gym clothes, ironed some shirts, polished my boots and was getting ready for some real R & R, a visit to downtown Ottawa, a city the likes of which I had never seen before. A trip past the parliament buildings was never complete without a stroll through to check the register of Canada's fallen soldiers. They turned a page every day. Somewhere in that book, Uncle Jack's name was recorded. He was Dad's younger brother and he fell in World War II. I never knew Uncle Jack, but somehow when I looked at that book, I felt a close kinship. I never missed an opportunity to check for his name.

Then, I'd head for a favourite watering hole that Mac had

recommended, the Bytown Inn. We sure didn't have anything like the Bytown Inn in Edson, and I really enjoyed sitting in the big soft chairs in the basement lounge. At suppertime, a big feed of Chinese at the Canton Inn was always high on the menu. I hadn't been in the east very long, but in the short time I was there, I had sure developed a taste for Chinese food, more specifically Cantonese. It was well rumoured that many Chinese used cat in their dishes and some of my new troop mates, those who were much more worldly than myself, kidded me about eating cat. That didn't bother me, for I was the guy with the cast-iron gut. I did wonder, though, why more people didn't use cat, for the food was very tasty. Then, if the money held out, I would return to the Bytown Inn. If not, I would cap the evening off with a movie and a bus ride back to the barracks. Man, but it was a great feeling to be so free and independent. I had never dreamed that life could be so grand.

But the best laid plans are not always to be. The tranquillity of the day was suddenly shattered. "48 Troop," barked a very authoritative voice. Every head in the room snapped to, eyes cautiously peering toward the big foyer in front of the two rooms that housed 48 Troop. "48 Troop. Fall out," the voice barked again.

"What gives?" I asked one of my troop mates who happened to be standing near the door. "This is Saturday and we're not on standby or anything. Are we?"

"Not that I know of," he replied. "But there's a corporal standing out there and he looks like he means business."

"48 Troop," roared the booming voice again. "I said to fall out and I mean fall out. Now!"

Reluctantly, I, along with several troop mates, scrambled

toward the door. There was no doubt about it. There was a corporal out there all right. He was dressed in full uniform, boots, breeches, tunic, shirt, tie, gloves, Stetson, riding crop and spurs. 48 Troop was not moving fast enough for his liking. "I said fall out, you horrible little men. When I say fall out, I mean fall out, and I mean fall out right now. Now, snap to it before I lose my good sense of humour."

"Sounds to me like he's already lost whatever he had," I mumbled, but very quietly as I raced down the stairs heading for the front of the barracks. For I remembered quite clearly both the parade square and the horse trough.

"Outside," he roared. "On the double now, lads. Let's go. Columns of three."

"Who is this guy?" I asked a troop mate as we bolted through the doors.

"Don't ask me," he mumbled. "I never saw him before in my life."

"I think I've seen him somewhere before," I replied. "But I can't put my finger on it."

There was an assortment of dress amongst those of 48 Troop who formed the ranks in front of the barracks that Saturday afternoon. Since no one was expecting to be called out, not all members of the Troop were present. Some were enjoying their freedom a lot more than this horrible little man. They had not dallied and were probably already enjoying the friendly confines of the Bytown Inn.

I cursed myself for being so slow. If I hadn't been in the habit of doing my chores before going out, I too would have been on my way. Now, I was stuck with some meaningless task, probably dunging out the stables again.

We were mustered in such a hurry no one had the opportunity to dress properly. Those who were being assembled presented themselves in the clothes they had been wearing. For some it was only a pair of shorts. To say the least, we were a motley-looking crew. A soon-to-be-frozen motley crew. It was at times like this that I knew I was a poor excuse for a human being. I had bolted through the door so fast that I had on sneakers and a pair of trousers, but no shirt, not even a T-shirt. "Man, I'd give my eye teeth for my short car-coat or even my white shirt," I mumbled. I stood there covered in goose-pimples about the size of walnuts and I shivered uncontrollably in the great outdoors.

"I'm Corporal Plank," he introduced himself. He strutted before the assembled troops like a peacock. We shivered, shook and froze. "As you know, lads, we are in the process of developing a new ride to represent the force in Canada and around the world. We take only the best horsemen, for the force takes a great deal of pride in presenting the best. This year, we are not going to be doing the Musical Ride on our tour. Instead, we will be presenting an exhibition ride. We will be putting our best horses and men on display before the world. Each man and horse will be completing a total of sixty jumps in eight minutes. There will be displays of individual horsemanship such as tent pegging. Anybody here know what tent pegging is?" he asked.

No one moved, no one said a word. Obviously no one knew what tent pegging was. "Well, don't worry about it," he tooted as he strutted back and forth. "There's plenty of time for that. Those of you who are fortunate enough to make the ride will learn soon enough."

Now I had a pretty good idea who this bird was. He was obviously with the ride. Everyone in the troop had heard about the new ride. They came into Rockcliffe at the same time as 48 Troop and had been riding every day since. I stared straight ahead, afraid to move even an eyeball as the corporal strutted back and forth for a few minutes. 48 Troop stood at attention. Each man was straight as a ramrod, frozen stiff, waiting anxiously for the next words of wisdom. I felt like saying 'tell us something we don't already know', but like the obedient servant I was becoming, I bit my tongue. This was one horrible little man who had a very good understanding of the consequences and the way I figured it, I had already said enough to last the whole nine months of training.

"Tell me, lads," he asked, being very polite. "How many of you fine men are riders?" I pinched the sides of my trousers with my fingers to keep from lifting my hand. I didn't need to draw any more attention to myself, but if he took shaking like a leaf for a yes, I was dead. "Good. Good, that's very good," he nodded and smiled. Obviously we had some riders in the troop. Or maybe we didn't. I wasn't sure, I couldn't see any hands, but he had seen something and whatever it was he seemed to be pleased.

"Now tell me, lads, how many of you have been properly outfitted for riding?" He paused and looked the length of the troop, waiting for an answer. He turned his head from side to side, searching for an answer that never seemed to come. "Well then, how many of you have been *fit for a saddle?*" he asked, and again his eyes searched the troop. "That's just what I thought," he stated in obvious disgust. He slapped a hand on his thigh and shook his head as if it were unbelievable that such an oversight could occur. "I don't know what this world is coming to," he mumbled and shook his head in disbelief. "I tell you, lads, if you don't do everything yourself, it just doesn't get done."

He paced back and forth saying nothing. As he strutted past me, I couldn't shake the nagging feeling that I had seen this guy before, but where? During the long, dreaded silence, while I shivered and shook, he stroked his chin, contemplating the next move. "Lads," he barked suddenly. "It's unfortunate that all of 48 Troop isn't here today, because this is going to be a very big day in your lives. A day you will long remember. Today, you are going to get the benefit of my years of experience. Each and every one of you are going to be fit for your very own saddle. I can't begin to tell you how important it is that each man's saddle be set up properly. Riding a horse is by no means an easy task and having the proper equipment adds a great deal to your ride. One day, you may have the pleasure of being asked to join the 'ride'. I only have one day for this, so I'm going to ask that you help your troop mates who are not here. Can you do that for me?" he asked, looking around the troop.

"Yes corporal," came the response from a few of the troop.

"Good. Good lads." He smiled, then turned. "Constable," he called to another member who had suddenly appeared.

"Yes corporal," he answered.

"Constable, you can take 48 Troop to the stables so that each man can be fit for a saddle."

"Yes, corporal. It would be my pleasure, corporal," came the eager response. And so, 48 Troop, those members not quick enough to have escaped, the fortunate lads who had been yanked from a very warm comfortable Saturday afternoon of leisure, were once more marched to the stables. There each man would be fit for his own saddle.

Once inside the stables, I shuddered as the troop was halted squarely in front of the horse troughs. Them I remembered all too well, for I could still see the deep blue eyes of a troop mate, staring up through the icy water from the bottom of the trough.

Man, it was cold and damp standing in that stable. I stood like a poor excuse for a human being, stiff as a pole, staring straight ahead at the beckoning horse trough. I could hear it calling: "Come on in, Bobby Adams. Come in, the water's fine!" Man, but I was starting to have a bad feeling way down deep in the pit of my stomach. I could not stop shivering and now, my goose-pimples seemed to have grown goose-pimples of their own.

In the cold, without my shirt, I started to sweat.

"Listen up, 48 Troop," sang the constable in a very friendly tone. Now here, I thought, was a good guy, a guy who was not overly impressed with his importance. "You will be called, one at a time, for your fitting. When you're called, you will fall out and follow me. The rest of the troop will continue to stand at attention until called. Is that clearly understood?"

"Yes, constable," came the unified response. This was it, I thought, as I braced myself. My name being Adams, starting with an A, I knew that I would hear my name called first. As usual I would be the first to experience the unknown.

I sweated bullets and waited for the word.

To my surprise, there were no names called. There was movement behind me as they picked the first guy. I could hear fading footsteps across the concrete floor. A door opened and closed, then all was quiet.

The constable continued picking guys off at random. One from here, one from there. Sometimes he even joked with them as they marched from the room. I stood there waiting, shivering and freezing as ranks got smaller and smaller.

Standing at attention, I had a lot of time to think. So far, training had not been all that I thought it would be, for I had not experienced the glamour I had been anticipating. I had not yet driven a shiny new patrol car, I hadn't fired my revolver, and my nice flashy red coat, the scarlet tunic, had yet to make an appearance.

My field trips had been nothing more than routine duties and sadly lacked the freedom I had envisioned. My experiences had been confined to shovelling snow, polishing brass, marching around outside and, of course, shovelling horse shit. So far I had conducted my own field trips, and they had nothing to do with the force. However, my field trips seemed to be lacking in imagination and variety, for they were highly focussed around the friendly confines of the Bytown Inn. The thrills of real field work, excitement and grandeur had so far eluded me.

But, although I resented this intrusion on my Saturday afternoon, I made up my mind not to rain on anyone's parade, at least not on this day. I did not relish the thought of trying to look up from the bottom of the horse trough. I, Constable Adams, was going to be one model recruit as I went through the saddle-fitting experience. Oh yes, I was going to be one cooperative fellow.

"You," the constable called and tapped me with a riding crop. I quickly took one pace forward.

"Adams here, constable," I called out loud and clear.

"Follow me, Adams," he replied. He gave me a big friendly reassuring smile, then turned and walked away. I marched briskly along, past the remaining troop mates. I was kind of surprised to notice that our ranks had diminished considerably. Those who had gone before had not returned. They're probably working on their tack right now, I chuckled. I could just picture happy young men rubbing saddle soap into the stiff leather and polishing the brass on the bridle. I was starting to feel much better as I followed him into the tack room. This was not the moment I had been waiting for since

97

I arrived, but it was none the less an important moment in my life. It was not the shiny new car or the fancy coat, but I had to admit my own saddle and horse would be a pretty good start.

I came to a snappy halt just inside the door and stood there, ramrod stiff, at attention. I heard the door click closed behind me.

"Stand at ease. Stand easy, lad," said the corporal, who was seated on a bale of hay. I stood easy and took the opportunity to look around at my surroundings. I could not get past the centre of the room. Immediately in front of the seated corporal I noted a sawhorse, a length of 2" x 4" lumber with legs nailed to it. On top of the sawhorse was a saddle. On either side of the saddle were two officers. I recognized them as constables, and they too seemed vaguely familiar. Then I noted the way they were squatted on their haunches. They reminded me of cowboys from a western movie. There was no doubt, these hardened veterans were probably from the ride. That was it, I had probably seen them with guys from the ride.

"Where you from?" asked the corporal.

"Alberta, corporal."

"Ah, from Alberta." He smiled a rather sinister smile. "Now, wouldn't you think that I already knew that?" he sneered. "I want to know from where in Alberta?"

"Edson, corporal," I hollered out loud and clear.

"Stand at attention when you address me," he suddenly roared. Immediately my body went rigid as I snapped to. My eyes stared straight ahead, at a wall covered in saddles. Then he turned to address the others in the room. "Edson," he mimicked me. "Isn't that nice, mama's boy here is from Edson?" he sneered. "And just where in hell is Edson?"

Man, I cursed myself for not getting out of the barracks

sooner. I did not like the sound of his voice. My saddle-fitting was starting to leave a very nasty taste in my mouth and I was getting awfully nervous and when I get nervous, I sweat. Little beads of sweat were beginning to dot my body again. "Near Jasper, corporal," I called out.

"Oh yes," he smiled, "western Alberta. You come from ranching country, constable. So I take it we have the honour of having a cowboy with us today? And I'll just bet you think you're a rider, too. Am I correct, Mr....?"

"No, corporal. I come from a farm and we only had skid horses on the farm."

"But, constable, I'm sure that you must have crawled up on a skid horse a time or two, didn't you?"

"Yes corporal, a time or two, corporal."

"Well then, what kind of a saddle did you use when you climbed up a time or two?" he asked. Now he was smiling again.

"Mostly I rode bareback, corporal," I replied.

"I'm not interested in how you rode," he snapped. "I asked you about the type of saddle you used."

"A western saddle, I think, corporal."

"A western saddle, mister. Did...did you say a western saddle?" he stammered like someone had just kicked him. "Western saddles are for sissies." I was really sweating now, especially the way he emphasized the s's with a lisp. "Well, mister," he crowed. "In the RCMP we use the English saddle. You really wouldn't know what an English saddle is, would you, mister?"

"No, not really, corporal," I replied, looking at the little patch of leather sitting on the sawhorse that made up the puny English saddle. There was no way that I was going to be familiar with anything at that moment. I quickly deduced that this was a learning experience and the less I knew, the better.

"That's what I thought," he crowed. "Well, mister, have we got a treat for you," he replied sarcastically. "In order for you to be fit for a saddle, you have to be sitting in it. But, you'll notice that unlike the western saddle, the English saddle does not have a saddle horn. Do you think that you'll be able to climb on without the help of a horn?"

"I think so, corporal," I replied.

"There's nothing for you to hang onto, mister. Are you sure you won't fall off? I wouldn't want you to hurt yourself." There was more laughter. The troops, even the friendly constable, were really enjoying this.

"Then what are you waiting for, man? Get on the damn thing. You're starting to test my patience, mister." I hesitated for a moment, then stepped forward. I straddled the sawhorse and sat down on the precarious perch.

"You'll have to put your feet in the stirrups so we can measure the length," advised one of the constables who was squatting on his haunches.

"I asked you a question," roared the corporal as I was lifting my feet to insert them in the stirrups. That booming voice scared me so bad, I lost my balance. With both feet in the air and clawing wildly for the stirrups, I began to list badly to one side. Instinctively I grabbed for a saddle horn that wasn't there. The saddle was twisting off the sawhorse. For the love of Pete, I moaned, I'm getting bucked off by a bloody standing sawhorse. Flailing around like a chicken with its head cut off, I was taking a nose dive for the concrete floor. Then a constable, one of the squatters at the side of the sawhorse, grabbed me and pushed me back up. Strong arms held me steady, then grabbed my feet and jammed them into the stirrups.

"Do you think I enjoy sitting here talking to you?" demanded the corporal.

"No corporal," I spoke up very loud to be sure that he heard. Now I had both feet planted firmly in the stirrups and I could feel the saddle shifting again. This time I was heading for the floor with my feet imbedded in the stirrups. I tried to kick the stirrups off, but they had been pushed on tight. My feet were locked in. Like a well-tied bundle I was headed for the floor when the other squatter came to my rescue. He grabbed me and pushed me back up to the top of the sawhorse. I wiggled and wobbled all over the place as I fought to stay upright.

"That's better," mumbled the corporal who seemed to be oblivious to my predicament. "You'd think that someone would teach these bloody recruits some manners. Ask them a simple question, and they ignore you. There's no respect anymore. No respect at all."

"Fifteen inches right stirrup," I heard one of the constables call out as I wobbled around. The corporal carefully made a notation on the clipboard.

"Fourteen and a quarter inches left stirrup," came the second constable's numbers. What gives, I thought, my left leg isn't three-quarters of an inch shorter than the right. What kind of a sorry excuse for a human being was I, anyway? I already knew that my arms were longer than they should be, but I always thought my legs were fine. I was thinking of the clerk who had made the mistake of telling Mom that I had a funny build and had regretted it. Now, I was having an argument with myself over whether or not I should dispute the length of my legs when I remembered the deep blues eyes in the horse trough. I quickly decided that if I could live with long arms, I could live with one short leg.

101

"You wanna try out for the ride, don't you, mister?" I heard the corporal roar and jerked to attention.

Surely this guy was kidding. After all this saddle fitting bull, he wanted to know if I, a horrible little man with weird measurements, wanted to be in the ride? I knew one thing for certain, if I hadn't hated horses and riding before this day began, I was certainly well on the way now. Being on the ride meant that I would have to be with horses every day. Early in the morning, all day long, all evening, seven days a week, working and riding with them and probably with this corporal. No way. It was out of the question. The ride was the last thing in the world I wanted to be on. My answer was an emphatic no. Then, I could not believe the words that popped out of my mouth. "Yes, corporal," I heard myself reply.

"Yes corporal, what?" he barked.

"Yes corporal. I'd love to be on the ride," I blurted out. What had come over me, why was I saying such things? I really didn't want to be on the ride.

"That's good," he smiled at me, obviously quite happy with my reply. "There's just one more thing, then. When you're on the ride, you have to be able to do many things in the saddle. For example, in tent pegging you will be carrying a lance and you have to be able to lean out of the saddle until your hand almost touches the ground." That part I believed for I had seen members of the ride practising the exercise. Meanwhile, here I was having trouble sitting upright in the saddle on the sawhorse and this yo-yo wants me to lean to one side. I breathed a sigh of relief when I heard him say, "We won't practice leaning in here, but we will need to see how far you can come forward in the saddle." He stood up and tapped his riding crop on the end of the sawhorse in front of me. "Do you think that you can get your head up this far?"

Suddenly, I thought of my dad. He had been a bronc rider. He had even ridden in stampedes. In fact, he loved horses. My dad wouldn't have hesitated or had second thoughts, he would have volunteered for the ride in a second. When I started out over the top of the saw horse, I wondered why had I even thought about not wanting to be on the ride. I could just picture myself on a magnificent mount, the saddle and the brass polished to a lustrous shine. I was in full uniform, red serge, Stetson, Sam Browne, breeches, boots, spurs and lance. It was a fabulous sight and Dad was there watching. I could see his smile, the smile of a very proud father.

As I slowly inched my butt out of the saddle and stretched forward, I decided that the ride was definitely for me. It was going to be a great field trip. I had a firm grip on the sawhorse and with my newfound enthusiasm for the ride, found that I was now far steadier as I worked my way forward, hand over hand. The closer my head came to the spot where the corporal was tapping his riding crop, the farther my butt came from the saddle. I was stretched right out, like an inchworm, both hands clasped tightly on the end of the sawhorse, my head held high over my hands. My mismatched legs were straight and my butt was way up, high in the air. I thought I had struck a pretty good pose when a noise suddenly cut though the air. I heard it plain as day. A whistling noise like something travelling through the air at a high rate of speed. WHIZZZZ, it whistled. Then there was this loud THWACK.

"What in the hell was that?" I started to mumble under my breath as it took a second to sink in. I hesitated for just a second before reacting. I didn't really feel it right away, but I knew what it was. Someone unseen had come up behind me and laid a healthy section of lumber across my arse. That slight hesitation with my butt in the air was a very tempting target. It allowed the swinger to reload and swing again. Once more the board whistled through the air. Everything was suddenly a blur as I hastily retreated to deposit my butt into the safety of the English saddle. But the second's hesitation and the movement were costly. My butt reached the saddle, but the board continued to whistle through the air. My feet were still lodged firmly in the stirrups. I lost my balance and once more headed for the floor head- first. This time, I felt the board and heard the sickening CRACK as it slammed across my back and ribs, driving me to the floor. Now, there were no friendly constables to catch the horrible excuse for a human being. With my extended arms and my mismatched legs I crashed in a heap to the concrete floor. My feet were still in the stirrups, and I was under the saddle and sawhorse.

Everyone in the room was doubled over laughing their guts out. That was a good one, I thought, Grandfather would have liked that one.

"Did you see that?" roared the corporal. "We got two whacks at the sucker before he fell out of the saddle."

Then it hit me, about as hard as the board. I looked up at the corporal, into the steely-blue evil eyes. He wasn't from the ride. He was from the senior troop.

My butt stung and my back hurt as I was ushered into another room and then out the back door, away from the remaining troop mates. "You get your sore butt back to the barracks and you keep your mouth shut if you know what's good for you," roared the evil-eyed man as he pushed me out of the stables.

Back at the barracks, several of my troop mates were nursing similar aches. For some reason, I didn't feel like spending what was left of my Saturday afternoon sitting. I stood by my bunk and looked around the room at the rest of my troop. Five guys, I thought, five cocky guys had taken the majority of my troop and picked us off one at a time. And we had lined up and waited for them to get to us. What a sorry-ass lot we were. Maybe the instructors were right; maybe we did have pea-sized brains.

48 TROOP

"Where's that useless piece of crotch rot?" roared the big burly recruit, a gorilla of a man who had suddenly appeared in the doorway of 48 Troop.

I looked up and the first things I noticed were the steely-blue eyes. I had seen those eyes before, at the horse troughing before 48 Troop was squadded, and they were there when I was fit for a saddle. They were mean evil eyes, not the eyes of a friend.

"There he is," yelled a lippy accomplice whose arm was wrapped over the gorilla's shoulder. He appeared to be attempting to squeeze his way into the room. He pushed and shoved his way forward, forcing the gorilla to take another step, then another into the room. But the lip did not want any part of the space out in front, he stayed behind the big fellow, the leader, the gorilla. "I see him," squawked the henchman again. "He's right back there, see him? That's the scum who screwed up today." With his free hand, he pointed past the gorilla at someone toward the back of our barracks room.

"Okay, let's get the mother," sneered the gorilla and started forward confidently. This little raid was to be another uncontested foray into the ranks of the junior troop to exact a measure of satisfaction. Members of a senior troop were only exercising their right, the right to dispense justice and discipline on the junior troops as they saw fit. The gorilla and his henchman were not alone; several of their troop mates had decided to partake in the cleansing and they surged through the door after them.

The invaders had entered one of the two rooms that our troop called home and by the sounds of their voices and the looks on their faces, they meant business. Like a pack of hyenas intent on their prey, they grouped to move forward. They had selected their victim, a troop mate. He was the person that had been identified as the screw-up. It was he who would be picked out of our midst and dealt with in the appropriate manner.

"C'mon, quit stallin'. Let's go and get this over with," called another voice as more members of the senior troop came through the door. Pushing and shoving, they followed the gorilla into the room.

"What in hell's going on?" asked one of my troop mates, as those of us in the room turned toward the intruders.

"You guys are harboring a piece of crotch rot in here, and he's giving us a bad name and we don't like it," snarled the gorilla. He stopped and surveyed the room, freezing everyone with a steely glance. Just enough threat there to make sure the lambs stayed put. Then he turned his head and laughed over his shoulder, "If these creeps had any guts, they'd take care of their own garbage. If anybody moves, you boys give 'em a dose of the same medicine I'm gonna give the screw-up." Then he turned and looked back toward the intended victim. "As senior troop, it's our duty to make an example of anybody that screws up. We're here to make sure he gets what's coming to him. In fact, just to make sure it's done right, I've decided to administer the medicine myself," he trumpeted confidently.

But apparently not all the lambs had been silenced by the stare as a voice called out, "I don't think so." It was the tone of his voice that seemed to be out of place for our group. A tone that seemed to carry as much authority as that of the gorilla leading the assault.

I had been sitting on my trunk, minding my own business, putting a spit-polish on my riding boots when all this commotion began. As the gorilla started forward, I started to stand up, but I, who had also been referred to as a disgrace to the force on several occasions, was not quite quick enough. From the corner of my eye, I caught a glimpse of a streaking form as a troop mate leapt off his bunk. Single-handedly he had risen to the occasion. Alone, if necessary, he would stand before the pack. He landed on the floor right beside me. Well actually, his path took him across a couple of bunks and over my trunk. Silly me, I stood up right in front of him. But obviously I, like the gorilla, was not much of an obstacle. My troop mate hit me with a tremendous body check and the impact sent me sprawling onto the floor at the feet of the gorilla and the advancing pack.

At that moment, I knew what a disgrace to the force was. It was me, groping around on the floor for my spit-shone boot, the one I had been slaving over, the one I dropped at the feet of the gorilla. My first thought was to save my boot and the shine, for every recruit knew the importance of a good shine. I knew the pack would understand my concern for the boot. "Hold it a minute, guys," I yelled. "Let me get my boot out of the way first." I reached for the boot just as the gorilla kicked.

This was incomprehensible, for nothing was more sacred than a good spit-shine. I watched in horror as the boot spun across the floor, the shining toe sending off little streaks of light as it skidded away. Then it cracked into a bed post, DING, the sound rang out and I could imagine the spit shine chipping like a piece of crystal. The boot came to rest wedged between a trunk and a bed post. This treatment of a freshly shone boot could only mean one thing: War!

Until this moment, 48 Troop had been a group of individuals. Each one of us, or so it seemed, had been trying to cope with the rigors of training, name-calling and the belittling as best we could within ourselves, by ourselves, for ourselves. There had been numerous incidents when a member of our troop had been brought to justice and made to answer for his sins by a senior troop member. We had all stood by and watched it happen. Heaven alone knew that I had firsthand knowledge of that fact. In the overall scheme of things, it was the responsibility of the instructor to teach and try to mold the troop into a cohesive unit. But it was the senior troops that set the example and if necessary, administered 'the medicine' for screw-ups. We had come to expect nothing more, nothing less. It was all part of training, part of the culture. I considered it to be nothing more than the way things were done.

My throwing up a road block in the face of my charging troop mate had been nothing more then a temporary distraction. He had quickly regained his balance and now stood before the advancing group. "No one comes into 48 Troop and teaches our crotch rot anything," I heard him shout defiantly.

Meanwhile, I, the poor excuse for a human being sprawled out on the floor at the foot of the gorilla, was a little more than ticked off with what happened over my hard-won spit-shine. I scrambled to regain my feet, to exact a measure of revenge, but suddenly, I found the room a little crowded. Gaining one's feet was not an easy task as bodies, friend and foe alike, pushed in from both sides. Several members of 48 Troop, my troop, had moved up behind my troop mate to meet the pack face-to-face. I began to have a feeling that I had never experienced before. This was no longer about me or my boot; it was about us, a comrade-in-arms under siege. It was about our troop. It was a feeling of oneness. It was everywhere in the room, with me and with my troop mate standing before the senior troop. It was infectious and spreading rapidly. Had we suddenly become a troop, a complete unit? We were reacting as one. Had my troop mate been responsible for this sudden change, this transformation from a group of horrible little men to a complete unit? I wasn't sure, but to say the least, I was somewhat taken aback by the quickness and ferocity of his sudden challenge.

"Says who?" sneered the gorilla staring down with those evil steely-blue eyes at the nose of my troop mate.

"Says this piece of crotch rot," my troop mate sneered back. I stared up in awe. From my ringlike seat on the floor at the feet of the rivals, I could see quite clearly. My troop mate was actually standing on his tiptoes trying to look the gorilla in the eye. "It'll take a big man to get through me," snorted my troop mate defiantly. After a short pause he added, "And I don't think you, or any of that slime you brought with you, are big enough." The challenge had been issued.

"I think 48 Troop are all a bunch of pukes," called someone from out in the hall.

"Who cares what you think, you bunch of pussies?" came a voice from behind me.

I had just about regained my feet, coming up between my troop mate and the gorilla, when out of nowhere I got some mail. "Get out of my way," growled the gorilla as he smacked me on the side of the head. Down I went again, crashing to the floor among the legs and feet, feet that repeatedly tried to stomp on my hands.

"I think we should teach the whole bloody bunch a lesson they'll never forget," I heard the gorilla roar as I sprawled on the floor for the second time.

Scrambling around on the floor was the exact sort of treatment that could definitely give a man a complex. I tried to avoid a million legs and feet that were milling around me. All seemed to be after my fingers. There was no room to stand up because the crowd was pushing in from both sides and over top. They kept forcing me down. To protect my hands and get up, I needed help. Being the ever-resourceful person I am, I found help. It was in the form of the closest big burly leg. I grabbed a hold of it and squeezing tightly, I started to haul myself up. But the gorilla took unkindly to this action, for it was his leg that I chose to climb.

"What the hell do you think you're doing?" he snarled. I had just about forced my way up to belt level when the gorilla suddenly stepped back. This must have been seen as a sign of retreat by my troop mates, who immediately surged forward. I was hit from behind, this time by my own troop mates, and again bowled over. I plowed headfirst into the gorilla, driving the top of my head into his crotch.

"Ooofff," he groaned and slumped forward, suddenly losing his wind and the will to rumble.

I don't know if it was me going down for the third time or him coming forward into the face of my troop mate, but instantly the room was turned into a battle zone. I hit the floor and was almost crushed by the weight of the groaning gorilla as he landed on top of me. The two troops came together in a mass of flesh. There were grunts, groans, curses and laughter as man struggled with man. Amid the thrashing bodies, beds and trunks were being tossed around like toys in a doll house as each man fought to gain the upper hand.

All around my head, feet and legs danced about. I was being kicked and stomped on by both sides. This horrible little man realized very quickly that he had better get up off the floor as he was in grave danger of being trampled to death. The gorilla was gone; he was nowhere to be seen by the time I finally pushed and shoved my way up between the struggling bodies. Instantly I found myself in the thick of the battle. Coming up between the two troops, one might say that I was caught in the middle, but not for long.

"Get that puke," someone yelled and willing hands from the senior troop gladly obliged. They embraced me, pushing, shoving, clawing, grabbing, kicking and gouging.

"Maybe I should have stayed on the floor and been trampled," I thought as the horde slowly inched toward the door. The door, the narrow opening, the only exit from the room was proving to be a more formidable obstacle than were any of the combatants. Bodies, hot, sweaty, sticky bodies, were suddenly pressed tightly together as the combatants inched their way out of the room. "Which one of you pussies forgot to wear deodorant?" I shouted as I fought against the surge.

"We'll show you who needs deodorant, you puke," someone growled in my ear. Then I felt my back being scraped across the door jamb. "How does that feel?" he laughed. "Here, want me to try that again?" he asked and I could feel him try to push me back into the room, but no luck. The slime from the senior troop was slowly being repelled, pushed into the foyer. There was no way back inside. The door jamb, the great equalizer, delivered the most bumps, bruises and scratches. Man, I was sure that every part of my body had been slammed into or scraped across the wood before we had finally fallen through the doorway. Out into the large foyer we struggled, rolling around and wrestling on the floor. One minute I was on the floor, with several bodies thrashing around on top of me; the next I was being yanked to my feet and dragged away. At times, as I was being manhandled around the doorway, this disgrace to the force felt like the only one doing battle, but out in the foyer there were several other groups. They too were locked in what appeared to be a life-and-death struggle.

Across the foyer we battled, crotch rot and disgrace to the force against slime and pussies, past the stairs and into the washrooms. The showers were like huge open troughs where several men showered at one time. They had been turned on earlier and were running full blast. The icy shower was the 'medicine' we had been promised. Several persons had already made it to the shower area ahead of us. Some had obviously received their dose of medicine. A number of bodies were thrashing around on the concrete floor. Some were trying to scramble out while others were pushing them back in. As we neared the water, more willing hands grabbed me and hoisted me into the air. They swung me back toward the toilets, then forward into the air, in an arc toward the showers. There were no more hands, no more clutching and grabbing, pinching and squeezing. I was floating, flying through the air, but not very gracefully, for my arms and feet were flailing and thrashing about trying to find a safe landing spot. I hurtled through the air, an uncoordinated missile. The icy cold water cut like a knife just before I crashed into the mess.

"Man is that water cold," I mumbled to the guy I landed on.

"Get off me, you creep," he growled.

I turned and looked directly into the steely blue eyes, the unfriendly face. The last time I had seen him, my head had slammed into his crotch and he landed on top of me. I couldn't help it. In the freezing shower, I started to laugh. "What's so funny?" he snarled.

"You, you big hunk of slime," I replied and rolled over in the shower holding my sides. "I guess you weren't as big as you thought you were, eh?"

This experience had suddenly become great sport. I was having a fabulous time as I tried to dodge another body that was being tossed into the fray. There were members from both troops in the shower. "What are you grinnin' about?" snarled the gorilla. He had crawled out of the mass of bodies and was laying on the concrete floor beside me. "You got tossed in, too. I don't see that you got somethin' to smile about."

"Oh yes I have. But you wouldn't understand," I chuckled, as I thought back to my first day in Rockcliffe when I had inadvertently witnessed the first of many senior troop justice dispensing sessions. They were sessions that I would long remember.

Yes, I thought, as I looked back at those steely-blue eyes and stood up, I may have gone in and I'm soaking wet, but I do have a reason to smile. The showers were still running full blast and bodies were still being tossed in as the gorilla struggled to get to his feet and limped out the door. I, for one, could not keep the smile off my face. I stood and watched as the gorilla started up the stairs. Very gingerly, he proceeded one short painful step at a time. Slowly he limped away to nurse his wounds and his injured pride. It was a crowning glory to the end of the battle.

I was soaked and chilled to the bone when I walked back into my room. I stopped and surveyed the scene. People had been busy while I was battling in the shower. Beds had been righted and trunks had been returned to their rightful place. My boot, which only minutes earlier had been wedged between a trunk and a bed post, had been retrieved and was sitting on top of my trunk. I looked to the back of the room for the troop mate who had been the object of the brawl. He was there, helping to straighten up. His clothes were dry. His hair was not messed up. He had not been touched. His troop mates had stood tall.

I couldn't wait for someone to try the next horse troughing, for we were a unit now. At last we were one. We were 48 Troop.

I KNEW EVERY DOORKNOB
IN TOWN

"Well, sir," I started to reply to the question being asked. It was mid-December and I had at last completed my training. Yes, this bit of sour cream had risen to the top and was detachment-bound. I had given a lot of thought to my future and where I would like to be posted. I had not wavered and the decision I made many months ago on the train ride across the Canadian Prairies was still with me. I wanted water, salt water. I wanted to feel the spray on my face. I wanted to wake up in the mornings and smell the ocean, to hear the waves splashing on the rocks, to taste the salt in my mouth and my nostrils. I wanted to walk, dressed in my red serge, on a boardwalk along the shores of the Pacific Ocean. "British Columbia, sir. I would really appreciate it if I could be posted to British Columbia. I think I've always wanted to live and work by the sea. Yes, British Columbia, that's my first choice, sir."

"I see, constable. So you prefer the ocean to dry land."

"That's right, sir," I replied. "The ocean, that's my

preference. I love the ocean."

"You're from Alberta, aren't you, constable?"

"That's right, sir. I'm from Edson."

"I take it then you've spent some time on the coast."

"Well, not really, sir," I replied hesitantly. "But I really like it by the ocean and, well, that's really where my heart is."

"What is your second choice, constable?"

"Well, I'd really prefer to go to B.C., but I'd go to the East Coast if I had to, just so long as I got to work by the ocean."

"So, you really want to go to sea, do you, lad?"

"Yes, sir," I replied happily.

"Tell me lad, have you ever been to the coast? Have you even seen the ocean?"

"No, sir," I replied.

"Very good constable, that will be all for today."

"Will I be going to British Columbia, sir?"

"I'll see what we can do, lad."

Interviews can really raise Cain with a man and they always made me real nervous. But not today, not this interview. Yes, when I walked through that door, I knew the gods were looking after me. Seated behind the desk was a face that I knew all too well, for it was I who was chosen regularly to care for his tack after he rode. Obviously I had done a pretty fair job and he had been pleased. Now, I was sure that he would remember me and my good work ethic. I was feeling pretty good about my interview. There was certainly no reason to believe that I wasn't going to be sent to the West Coast. Failing that, to the East Coast.

A few days later, I, along with the rest of my troop mates, had received the good word and we were dispatched across the length and breadth of Canada. Everyone was talking excitedly about their posting. When I first received my orders,

I thought there must be some mistake. The letter "E" would signify that I was going to British Columbia, however the "E" on my orders looked suspiciously like an "F". I had to search my memory to find out where "F" Division was. British Columbia I knew was "E" Division, so "F" had to be close. Alberta was "K" Division and Saskatchewan was...oh no, Saskatchewan was "F" Division. I was about as far as you could be from the ocean and still be in Canada. Saskatchewan was dry; dry Saskatchewan. The only salt in the air would be off the alkali sloughs that are everywhere in Saskatchewan.

It was a brand new year and I was the newest member of the team, the junior man in the Humboldt, Saskatchewan RCMP detachment. I was up before the sun, which isn't hard to do in Saskatchewan in early January. I was full of vim and vigour, full of enthusiasm, ready for my first official shift as I strutted out of my newly assigned bedroom, my first real home since Rockcliffe. I marched across the hall and entered the RCMP detachment office. I was pumped, ready to receive my orders and meet the challenges of the day. This is what I had really signed on for, working on detachment. I could hardly wait to commence with the field work, to hit the streets, to fight crime and/or evil. I had to admit, Saskatchewan was not British Columbia and the endless miles of snow-covered prairie were not the endless waves of the Pacific Ocean, but I knew I'd find my boardwalk and strut my stuff. With a smile as wide as the great Saskatchewan prairies I strode into the detachment office.

"Well, look what we have here," chuckled the corporal, appearing to be somewhat amused. The corporal had been around, he had seen this before. I wondered how many times he had seen the rosy cheeks of a rookie reporting for duty. "It looks to me like you survived your first taste of the prairies?"

"You betcha," I replied as if it were nothing and chuckled along with him. Then I hastily added "Corporal." I had almost committed the cardinal sin. "Constable Adams, reporting for duty, corporal," I quickly added and snapped to attention.

"I think we've already met," he joked. "And forget that," he waved his hand to brush off the stiff stance. "Relax, lad, we don't need all that formal stuff around here. But tell me, Constable Adams, don't you think that maybe you're just a tiny bit early for your shift?"

"Not me, corp," I replied enthusiastically. "I'm here now and I'm ready...ready to go to work. I'm reporting for duty."

"That's good, lad," he chuckled. "You're eager, enthusiastic, chewin' at the bit, itchin' to get goin'. I admire that in a man."

"Thanks, corp," I smiled. Man, had I made a good impression. In the silence that followed, I had all sorts of visions. I knew that in a few minutes I was going to be handed an important case to solve. I could picture myself travelling to the crime scene, across the flat prairie, in a brand new cruiser.

"Have you checked the duty roster?" he asked.

"Duty roster?" I replied. "What's that?"

"That's what tells you when you work, when your shift begins and ends. Do you see that desk and typewriter up near the counter?"

I looked back through the door. There were three desks, all in a row. They were in the exact same places as when I had first arrived. One thing was different, though. The desk that was right up at the front, the desk closest to the counter, had an empty wire basket sitting beside the typewriter last night. Now, the wire basket was no longer empty, it was loaded with a mountain of paper. "Yeah," I replied. I was starting to get a message just by looking at all the paper.

"Well lad, on top of that desk you will find a duty roster. You go and check it out and I'm sure you'll find your name on it."

My walk to the desk was not near as brisk as it had been when I entered the office. That mountain of paper seemed to get bigger and bigger as I got closer. Sure enough, on the very top of the mountain was a duty roster and it did have my name on it.

"Graveyard," I moaned. "You gotta be kidding! I can't believe I'm working the graveyard shift."

"Look at it closely, lad. You'll see when you start with the graveyard shift, it only gets better."

He was right. One week of graveyards, followed by one week of days, followed by one week of afternoons, followed by one week of graveyards....It was an endless cycle.

"You go on and have yourself a good day's sleep now," he laughed. "Come back in around ten tonight and one of the boys will show you around."

"The graveyard shift," I muttered to myself. I looked out the window and on the eastern horizon could see the faint streaks of dawn. I turned around and slunk out of the office like a whipped pup. It wasn't even daylight yet and already I felt like I had been kicked out of the office. Whoever said that I was lucky to be assigned to a detachment had to have a hole in his head, I thought as I plunked my butt onto my bunk. Alone in the dingy little room, I tried to sleep, but with the detachment office right across the hall I heard the phone ringing and the clackity-clack of an old Underwood typewriter as someone pounded on the keys. I heard voices, laughter, cursing, singing. I heard absolutely everything that went on. Sleep would not come and I longed to be part of the action across the hall. Then I remembered that mountain of paper on the first desk. On second thought, maybe I didn't really want to be that much a part of the action.

I met my mentor around six that evening. I hadn't been able to sleep and decided I would get a head start on my learning. He was a constable like myself, and although senior to me, he too was a junior man.

"You're on town detail, just like me," my mentor advised me later that evening when I questioned him about getting to the real police work. I was itching to get into that car and make my mark.

"What does that mean?" I asked.

"It means you get to work all your shifts in town, just like I do," he chuckled.

"Not me," I stated, for I knew something he didn't. I had inside information. "I'm here to do real police work, detachment work. I don't think that I'll be seeing too many graveyard shifts."

"That's good," laughed my mentor. "You let me know how you make out. In the meantime, why don't you go and grab your duds and come with me? I'll introduce you to the doorknobs. Then I'll fill you in on the duties that the rest of us peons have to perform on the late shift."

I figured that something had struck him as being very funny, for he was having a good laugh and just shook his head as he walked over to a large walk-in vault, spun the combination, swung the heavy door open and walked inside. Meanwhile, I retrieved my gear from my room and returned to the counter and waited. My mentor was pretty excited when he returned with his Sam Browne and revolver. "I couldn't find your handgun in there," he informed me, unable to mask his concern.

"It was in my room with me where it belongs," I replied unconcerned.

"What do you mean where it belongs? What the hell is it doing in there?" he asked like he couldn't believe what he was hearing.

"That's where I keep it," I informed him. "Where it's nice and handy if I need it."

"Well, not anymore you don't," he replied. "Around here, handguns and ammunition are kept in secure storage. If you know what's good for you, when you finish your shift, you'll put that thing in the safe and keep it there the same as everybody else does. I'd also suggest that you better not let the corporal find out where you've been keeping that."

"Whatever you say," I shrugged.

Before heading out, I donned my latest uniform issue, the huge buffalo coat that came with the Saskatchewan posting. The coat, covered with long shaggy hair, was extremely bulky and very heavy. It felt like I had pulled the entire buffalo on as the weight settled over my shoulders. I'm sure I resembled a hairy Sumo wrestler, emitting the very distinct aroma of moth balls as I waddled across the office to the door. I had to turn sideways to get through the door and my bulk filled the hall. Outside on the street, the sidewalk was another matter. It was impossible for two buffalo coats to walk side by side. I thought it would be important to show a united front and I tried to walk beside my partner. To the untrained eye, I'm sure it appeared that two huge bears were wrestling as we jostled along.

My partner said little. He had staked out his share of the sidewalk and walking next to the buildings he maintained a steady course. I, on the other hand, zigged and zagged, moving in and out, dodging penny metres, ducking under sign posts or stepping around telephone poles. I danced along the sidewalk like a love sick buffalo as I continually jockeyed for position.

Finally, I conceded that there was only room for one of us on the sidewalk. I dropped back and followed along like an obedient servant. Through the streets and back alleys of Humboldt, I humped along. Where adequate width allowed, I moved up and walked along one step to the right and a good step to the rear; otherwise I followed in his path. I watched as he reached forward at each doorway and heard the rattle of the doorknob as we moved down main street.

"What have you been shown so far?" asked my mentor. We had just entered the first alley and he whipped out the biggest silver flashlight I had ever seen. He flicked the switch and a big beam lit up the way. I had pulled out the little two-cell job I had and flicked it on. A small orange ray coloured the snow. I quickly switched it off before my partner saw it. I stuck it back into the pocket of the buffalo coat.

"Nothing," I replied as I stepped over to the other side of the alley and moved up to walk closer to him.

"Nothing?" he asked. "I thought you made the rounds New Year's Eve?"

"Yeah, I did, but nobody told me what to do, so I just walked down the street and checked the doors."

"What were you looking for?"

"I don't know. I guess to see if they were open," I replied.

"How many times did you make your rounds that night?"

"I checked them a couple times, I guess."

"A couple times? You mean that no one told you that each door has to be checked at least four times a night by the man on graveyard shift?"

"Nope," I replied. "That's probably because I'm gonna be on detachment."

"Well, until you get on this detachment of yours, why don't I just show you where every front, side and back door to every business is located. Just in case you have some spare time and lower yourself to help out those of us less blessed then yourself," he chuckled.

"Show away," I replied.

Shaking doorknobs in the middle of the winter in the little town of Humboldt, Saskatchewan was really not my idea of a field trip. In all my dreams of glory, there had not been any visions of walking up and down main street and tiptoeing through the back alleys rattling doorknobs in the middle of the night. But every third week I found myself on the graveyard shift, and often late in the afternoon shift, doing exactly that.

I don't think that if I really tried, I could have found a more boring job. I even tried to make a game of it. I studied each doorknob. I learned which ones to push in and which ones to yank on to make sure they were secure. Some doors were solid, tight against the jamb, others rattled like crazy and often threatened that with just a little effort they would release. It was not long before I knew just how much resistence each offered. There was no doubt, with what I knew, my career would blossom and grow on the doorknobs of Humboldt.

As the nights stretched into weeks, my dreams of real field trips started to fade. Unlike the days that were getting longer, the chances of a real field trip seemed to be getting shorter. But as I trundled through the alleys along side fences and outbuildings, I did begin to notice little changes. Here and there cracks in the boards or protruding nails seemed to be growing hair. Closer observation revealed they were little tufts of buffalo hair. Obviously I or one of my detachment mates was passing too close to these hazards and slowly the buffalo coats were being stripped of their finery. I made a mental note to steer clear of protruding nails and cracks in boards or one day my warm buffalo coat would be nothing more then a strip of buffalo hide.

But every activity has its moments, moments that replace hours of tedious boredom with minutes of sheer panic. Shaking doorknobs was no exception.

One night I had completed the first tour of the main streets and back alleys of Humboldt. I had renewed my acquaintance with all the doorknobs and confirmed that all were safely secured. Around one in the morning, on the second tour, I had rattled the knobs on all of the front doors. Finding them secure, I turned my attention to the back doors of the businesses off of main street. As I approached the back door of one business, my heart skipped a beat. I noticed before I got close that the door was slightly ajar. It wasn't opened very far, but even I couldn't have missed the wisp of vapour from the warm air from the interior escaping through the crack. It trailed off into the night. My heart began to race. This was what I had been trained for, been waiting for, real police work. I had just discovered my first break-and-entry.

The complacency that had become so much a part of my nightly routine was suddenly shattered. Slowly, with a great deal of enthusiasm, I approached the door. This horrible little man was going to nab a passel of bad guys.

Then I started to think, but thinking at a time like this could be a bad thing. Do what you were trained to do, my head kept telling me. But the question was, what had I been trained to do? Why, I had been trained in the proper method of checking doorknobs and it was an activity that I was superb at. I could breeze through the checking of doorknobs with my eyes closed, and often did. But here, in the middle of the night, in a dark alley, an open door, this was a whole new ball game. In all my months of training, no one had ever told me what to do if and when I encountered an open door. Maybe I had better think about this a little, I thought before I proceeded any further.

"Should an open door be a problem?" I asked, starting a little conversation with myself. "Not really," I replied. "After all, I am a policeman, I have been trained as one of Canada's finest. I am the cream of the crop and should be prepared to deal with the unexpected."

During the conversation, I had covered the remaining ground between myself and the door. I stood there at the back of the building, beside the door, and wondered what do I do next? I had been trained not to stand in front of the door, open or closed. Bad mail could come through the door without warning. Standing beside that open door was a whole new nerve-wracking experience. I tried to get a look inside without being seen. I knew I was confronting the unexpected. "Why didn't this happen last week on one of the other guy's shifts?" I mumbled as I tried to prepare myself to meet the challenge. Slowly I peeled off my gloves and decided to replace the weak beamed flashlight with my revolver.

I realized that my hand was soaking wet from sweat when I loosened the holster flap and slid my hand over the grip of my Smith and Wesson .38 Special. This I did very slowly and deliberately. I was determined not to make a sound of any kind. I would not alert the intruder to my presence. Then I started to worry; had I made any noise coming down the alley? Man, I couldn't remember if I had been whistling or not. Whistling was something that I often did. I made a mental note: If I live through this I certainly won't be whistling again.

That I could count on.

Cripes, I thought, as I carefully slid the revolver from its holster and listened, the bloody gun will probably slip from my sweaty hand and fall in the snow. I wasn't sure whether I should concentrate on hanging onto the gun or listening for burglars. There was no sound to be heard and I gently pushed the door open. I needed a better look at the interior of the building and prayed that the hinges wouldn't squeak. Ha. This must be my lucky day. It was a well-oiled door, it swung open without a trace of sound. A cloud of condensation burst forth as the warm and cold air mixed in the doorway. As I peered into the building, I suddenly realized that I couldn't have seen anybody if I wanted to.

I peered long and hard through mist and thought that I could make out a long hall leading from the back of the building towards a large open area at the front. There were no lights at the back of the building, but the streetlights at the front shone through the large windows and illuminated the front office. The mist gave the inside of the building a haunting glow that swirled and danced. Through the haze, I figured that I could see right through to the front street. I was relieved to see that the hall was empty. No one there, but inside, somewhere, someone was lurking, waiting for me. I could just feel it.

On each side of the hall I could see darkened shadows. Now my mind was really working overtime and my heart was slamming around in my chest as I paused at the back door and listened for a noise, any noise at all. "Please," I prayed. "If you're in there please make a noise." But there was no noise, no movement, only deathly silence. I felt the night closing in around me.

Very carefully I stepped through the doorway and pulled

the door in behind me. I noticed that each of the darkened shadows was a door. All were open, some more so than others. I started to inch my way forward when I heard this terrible sound. Something was scraping on the wall. I stopped and listened...nothing. When I started to move again, the scraping started. It took me a while to figure out that it wasn't anything more then the hair on the buffalo coat. The hair touching the wall sounded to me like someone scratching their fingernail on a blackboard. I moved to the middle of the hall and continued, pausing after every step, listening for sounds and imagining all sorts of them. Everything was magnified. I was being extra careful to put my feet down slowly. I cursed the leather soles and myself for not wearing overshoes on this night. I prayed that I did not make a sound on the tile floor, but even my carefully placed feet sounded to me like I was stomping through the barn.

I inched my way up to the first set of doors, one on each side of the hallway. I had to choose which one to look into. If I chose the wrong one and the intruder was in the other waiting for me, I'd be blown away. I'd never know what hit me. I had to make a decision and already I didn't like the choices. A little voice inside my head said, "Check to the left first." So, for no good reason, I carefully peeked around the door jamb and looked into the darkness on the right. It's blacker then the inside of a cow at midnight, I thought. I couldn't see a bloody thing. Maybe the door to the left would be a little better. I pulled back and inched my way back across the hall and peeked in. Same thing, it was too dark. I couldn't see a thing. So much for the little voice. It didn't know any more then I did, I thought. Now I only hoped that when I passed in front of them that someone wasn't waiting in there who could see me in the hall.

This, I thought, was the ideal way to get shot, passing in front of two open doors and once more my mind started to play games. Then I started to think stupid things, like....Thank God I put on clean shorts when I started my shift. Mom would absolutely die if I got shot and was taken to the hospital wearing dirty shorts. My heart was still pounding as I thought about some past missed opportunities and swore that if I lived through this day....

I shook my head. Man, a guy really had some stupid thoughts running through his head at a time like this. I quit thinking and worked my way past the two doors, then thanked the good Lord there had been no shots. I had just come even with the second set of doors and was once again trying to decide which door to try first. Once more the little voice in my head said "Check to the left." I listened and I slowly peeked around the door jamb on the left. That was better, I thought, this room has a window in it and enough light shone through from the outside to allow me to see shapes and objects. I was congratulating myself on my fine choice when....

POP...POP...POP...POPPRRRRRR! The sound exploded like a series of cannon shots. They reverberated throughout the building. I just about filled my drawers. My heart leapt into my throat and my pulse boomed in my ears. "You dummy!" the little voice screamed at me. "You chose the wrong door! You're dead meat." The cannonading blasts came from the door on the right.

I hadn't felt any bullets crashing into my body. With the sounds still echoing in my ears I instinctively swung my revolver in the direction of the sound that had emanated from the door on the right and at the same time screamed into the darkness. "Don't move...or I'll shoot!"

Now my heart was really pounding and if I thought I was

sweating before, it was nothing to the rivers of water cascading under the buffalo coat and running down my body. Now fear screamed in my ear. "SHOOT! SHOOT! You idiot, SHOOT, before he shoots you." But try as I might I could not summon enough strength to pull the trigger. The revolver was pointing into the dark, at what, I had no idea. The room was pitch black and I couldn't see a bloody thing in there. I was frozen, scared stiff, standing in a dark hallway looking into an even darker room.

Slowly my eyes started to adjust and with the very faint amount of light from the window in the office across the hall I could just make out two white objects. They were about even with my pistol. Were they attached to something, someone? I wondered. Slowly an outline began to take shape. It appeared to be a person. He appeared to be in a crouching position right in front of me. Again something from deep within me screamed. "SHOOT! SHOOT!" But once again, I was so bloody scared I could not pull the trigger.

If it was a person, I thought it was not moving. I squinted to get a better look, but it didn't help. Whatever it was, it was sitting as still as a statue. The two white objects appeared to be looking back in my direction, at the business end of my .38 Special. The sneaking and being extra quiet was no longer an issue. I reached up and fumbled for the light switch and flicked it on.

I just about died when I saw that the barrel of my revolver was about six inches from the two white objects. Eyes. Big round eyes that showed nothing but gut-wrenching fear. Fear from the revolver shoved in his face. Fear from the big hairy being completely blocking the doorway. Fear on the face of a man who had his pants down around his ankles and was sitting on the toilet, shaking like a leaf. Maybe he didn't even see me standing there, I thought as I took a close look at him. His eyes were literally crossed as they homed in on the muzzle of the revolver that I was holding in front of his face. I'm not sure who was more scared, him or me. In addition to him being scared, he was also very drunk, but he was rapidly sobering up as he stared doom in the face. I thought that he could be a ghost, his face was so pale.

"Get your hands over your head," I yelled with all the authority I could muster. He lifted his hands slowly, not taking his eyes off the revolver. "Now stand up," I barked again. As he started to stand I realized that his pants were still down around his ankles. "On second thought, you better stay sitting," I barked again. "Who's in here with you?"

"Just me," he slurred. "I'm all by myself."

"What the hell are you doing in here?" I asked again, even though his immediate actions were quite evident.

"I'm the owner," he replied meekly. "It's my place. Please don't shoot me. I just had to go the bathroom so I just stopped in for a minute."

Piecing together the story, I learned that he was indeed the owner and had been out on the town doing a little celebrating and over the course of the evening had tipped one too many. Actually, he had tipped several too many, but he had been smart enough not to try to drive and was walking home when the call of nature gave him an urgent message. In response to this sudden need, he had stopped at his place of business. However, in his haste he had left the back door unlocked and open. He had been quietly sitting on his throne going about his business when I discovered the open door and began my search of the premises. He stated that he had not heard a thing as I entered the building and started down the hallway. Given his condition, that was not surprising. The sudden loud noise I heard and reacted to was nothing more than the amplified sound of gas being passed into a toilet bowl. It had simply been extremely bad timing on his part. He had chosen the very moment that I was passing the door to the can to pass gas. That fart, the natural act of passing air, came very close to having a serious impact on both our lives. As it was, it cost me about twenty years of my life and I could just imagine trying to explain to a judge and jury how I had single-handedly shot a drunk off a crap can.

I don't mind saying, it was one badly shaken poor excuse for a human being who now had a very healthy respect for shaking doorknobs that continued with his field trip, down the back alleys of Humboldt, Saskatchewan.

THE METER MOUNTIE

Spring had finally come to the prairies. Like the rest of the prairie animals who had survived a long cold winter, I too shed my winter coat. The long-haired shaggy buffalo coat, with the hair that was not hanging on a nail or wedged into a crack in a board in some back alley, had been retired. It would spend the summer hibernating in a box surrounded by a million moth balls. The ever-lengthening spring days were a welcome change to the dreary days of winter. I was looking forward to my first summer as I anticipated the prospect of real field trips. I looked hungrily out at the prairie. Somewhere out on that flat surface there was serious crime anxiously waiting for an enthusiastic, gung-ho young horse cop to ride in and solve. I watched the prairie awakening, arising from a blanket of snow. I watched as it donned its summer coat of green. I watched the ducks and geese flying overhead in huge flocks, moving out across the country as they returned from their southern home. I watched, I waited and I dreamed of field trips away from town, out in the country where the action was.

One Monday morning, I arrived at the office following a rare Sunday off. Monday was shift change day, and once every three weeks, I got to work day shift. This Monday, being the third week, I, the junior constable on detachment, was starting my week of day shifts. I really savoured the day shifts, for it was the one week that I did not have to prowl around the back alleys shaking doorknobs.

On the top of the paper in my basket was a small, thick booklet. I picked up the item that had mysteriously made its way to my desk. I flipped open the cover and inside I counted twenty-five small ticket-type documents. The back copy of each ticket was a small envelope that contained the same information printed on the outside. The book also contained one piece of carbon paper firmly anchored at the back. "What's this?" I asked.

"That? Oh, that's a book of meter tickets," one of my co-workers advised me. "It appears that you've been neglecting some of your duties," he continued. "You seem to forget that you're not on detachment here, you're on town detail. Now, on town detail when you work day shift, you check parking meters. When someone forgets to feed their meter, you write them one of those little tickets. That shouldn't be too hard for a bright young fellow like you to grasp, should it?"

"Really!" I replied. I could hardly believe my ears. Not in my wildest imagination had I ever dreamed that one of Canada's finest would walk the streets checking meters. "You gotta be kidding me, right?"

"Wrong," he dead-panned.

"You mean I've graduated from shaking doorknobs to writing parking meter tickets?"

"No, you haven't graduated from anything," he laughed. "You shake doorknobs on the graveyard shift and check meters on the day shift and when you're not doing that, you sit in here and do paper work. That's what town detail does."

"Don't they have meter maids or something like that in this town?" I asked.

"You can bet on it," he laughed. "And you're it. You're the meter Mountie."

Well, I'm sure glad I survived ten months of training and learned how to ride a horse in preparation for this challenging assignment. If for one minute I had thought that shaking doorknobs in Humboldt was a mundane, useless endeavour, it was only because I had yet to commence my duties as a meter maid. I had never paid much attention to the meters that graced the streets in front of the businesses in Humboldt. To me they were only markers that identified the individual parking spaces.

I sat there, reading the information on the ticket and the envelope. "Is this for real?" I asked. "You mean to tell me that for the privilege of parking in the business section of downtown Humboldt each person is required to feed the meter one penny? One big fat penny? And, if a guy hasn't got a penny, he gets a one-dollar ticket?"

"That's one thing about you, son, you catch on fast," chuckled my co-worker.

Because I had been negligent in my meter duties and to insure I mastered this weighty task, I was assigned to one of the senior constables for a leisurely morning stroll along the streets of Humboldt. Thus began my second round of introductions. This time it was to the meters, for it was important that I knew the hiding place of each and every meter. As we strolled along the streets of Humboldt, my mentor either tapped each meter on the top with a pen or pointed out their location. None appeared to be that hard to find since they were all cemented firmly onto the edge of the sidewalk. There was probably more danger of impaling oneself on a meter then in missing it. But, I had to admit that this field trip, conducted in light of day in the sunshine, was preferable to the late-night door checks.

"We wrote close to one hundred tickets last year," I was informed as we worked our way through town. "That's the most meter tickets that have been written here so far."

Somewhere in our wanderings we approached a car where the total red colour of the meter flag indicated that the penny had not been paid or had expired. Immediately I laid pen to paper. I recorded the date, the time, the meter number, the make and colour of the car and the licence plate number on a ticket. Then I painstakingly extracted the little envelope from the pad and placed it under the windshield wiper on the driver's side of the vehicle. "How's that for efficiency?" I asked, standing back to admire my work. I had just completed my first meter ticket under a very watchful eye. I was pretty happy that I had found a violator on this trip. I felt it was important that I performed this task right here and now in front of my mentor. Now, I was going to get the much-needed feedback.

"Not bad for a rookie," he smiled and I smiled, too, waiting for the next words of wisdom. "Not bad at all. But one thing you should know," he cautioned. "We ticket everybody except the mayor. His car doesn't get a ticket, remember that."

"Right," I replied. "I'll remember that." As he turned to walk away, I realized that I had received about as much feedback as I was going to get. "What makes the mayor's car so special?" I asked, remembering my training and my duty to treat all persons the same, without fear, favour or affection.

"He uses his car on town business, so he's exempt. And you should also know that it really ticks the corporal off when he has to cancel tickets," he replied and lifted his eyebrows, giving me a funny little look as we walked on.

"So tell me, how do I know the mayor's car from any other car? Does it have a sign on it saying mayor or something?"

"No, no. There's no sign on it, but it does look suspiciously like the car you just tagged. Now if I was a young buck lookin' to get on the corporal's good side, I'd have a good long look at that car. You'll probably be seeing a lot of it before the summer's over," he chuckled.

I turned and took a good look at the car with the ticket on the windshield. So, that's what the mayor's car looks like. I made a mental note to make sure that I would recognise it on future field trips along the metered streets of Humboldt. I was so intent on making sure I had a picture of the mayor's car etched in my mind that I walked right into a meter that suddenly stepped in front of me. "Oooff," I moaned as I gasped to catch my breath. "Dang, that smarts."

"You should really watch were you're goin'," cautioned my mentor. "There's nothing more embarrassing then a policeman draped over a penny meter."

"Tell me, how often do I have to go on these meter patrols?" I asked as I turned and took a last look at the little envelope under the windshield wiper. How long would it be before that came back to haunt me, I wondered?

"Carry the book with you. Every time you walk down the street, if you see a red flag in the meter, write the ticket. It's not complicated."

"Right," I replied. Unless, of course, it's the mayor's car, I thought. "I can agree with that, but I really have to question all this for a penny. Surely we've got better things to do with our time then worry about penny meters, haven't we?"

"You don't," he answered matter-of-factly. "Remember, we have a town contract here, and you're on town detail. You're also the junior man, so for now, you get the meters. Have fun and try to remember the mayor's car."

I had been doing an awful lot of filing during my fling on the graveyard shift and hadn't seen any of these little tickets floating around. Possibly it was one more thing that I had been negligent of. "I don't recall seeing any of these little suckers floating around in the filing," I asked. "Why's that?"

"I guess we must have saved them for you," he laughed.

After my introduction to meters and the great art of meter ticket writing, I was released on an unsuspecting public. I didn't stop for coffee that afternoon. Instead I opted for a field trip. I, the meter Mountie, was going to check my latest charges. It became obvious very quickly why I hadn't seen any meter tickets. It didn't appear that the citizens were very concerned that any tickets would ever be written. I hadn't travelled far on my field trip when I came across the first violator. I slapped an envelope on that offending vehicle so fast, it would make a person's head swim. Then, I found another and another. The meters were not being fed their penny; they were starving. The town of Humboldt was full of penny-pinching violators. Now, this was a field trip that a person could enjoy, I chuckled as I wrote, tore and slipped little envelopes under windshield wipers. This was not just any field trip, it was an extended field trip and it was paying dividends, big dividends. A buck an envelope. That buck was big money to a second class constable. I was out of the office and I checked each meter several times that afternoon as I walked and I wrote.

On my second round of meter-maiding that afternoon, I began to notice little things. The one that caught my eye and immediately registered was the gatherings in the windows. I seemed to be a pretty popular fellow, particularly with the ladies who pressed toward the window to watch a dollar ticket being placed on the windshield of a car. I would smile to each gathering and tip my hat as I left the scene and strutted to the next vehicle.

I was so deeply engrossed in bringing these violators to justice that I must have forgotten one important bit of information. "We ticket everybody except the mayor. His car doesn't get a ticket, remember that," my mentor had cautioned me. For some reason that warning had slipped my mind. It blew right through the space between my ears.

I was so busy writing that I had not paid any particular attention to the many cars I ticketed that first day. But obviously, during the course of my travels, I had found the mayor's car. The next morning, I found myself standing before the corporal's desk. I watched as he thumbed through a stack of meter ticket envelopes. I watched him pause, take a deep breath and sigh, then shake his head as if what he was seeing was unbelievable. Then he would extract that envelope and flick it towards me. The corporal was a good shot when it came to flicking envelopes, for it would land on an ever-growing pile of envelopes. According to the stack of tickets and the corporal, I had found the mayor's car on several occasions. I didn't really think that there were that many envelopes in the pile, but I was assured that one was one too many.

The corporal sat me down for a long fatherly talk which

he concluded with, "Adams, I don't want to see another ticket cross this desk that was placed on the mayor's car. Is that clear?" he sighed.

"Gotcha, corp," I replied. I had been around long enough to call him corp and to know when he meant business. I assured him that I would do my best.

Now, I loved to be outdoors, especially the outdoors on a bright day when the sun was shining, and I took advantage of every opportunity to skip out of the office. I did not, however, enjoy the role as the meter Mountie. I hated that part of the job. I hated looking into the little face on the meter to see if it was red. I hated writing a ticket for a neglected penny. And I was beginning to have doubts about what had originally seemed to me to be a fan club. The ladies who clustered around the windows as I patrolled the meters appeared that they were more into pointing and laughing than admiring. Yes, before long I particularly hated it when people would gather in the window and watch the meter Mountie place an envelope on a windshield. Being a meter Mountie was not the glory I had anticipated. I was not in my nice red coat, this was not the boardwalk and these folks were not the admiring crowd of lovesick girls I had dreamed of. Checking meters was a waste of the talents of a fine investigator such as myself. My talents could be better utilized out in the district, patrolling the countryside, searching out illegal stills and finding hardened criminals. But for now the meters were the only justification for extending any trip and the more tickets I wrote, the longer I stayed out. I endured the pain.

There was something about the mayor's car. I had that baby aced, I even saw it in my dreams, but for some reason, I had a mental block where that car was concerned. When that car and I met at a meter, the make, model and licence plate number, well, they always seemed to escape me. The mayor's car was like a pot of honey and I was drawn to it like a fly every time I hit the street. According to the corporal, I, for some incomprehensible reason, "laid a completely unreasonable amount of paper on that car. Now you're a bright young fellow," snorted an irritated corporal. "For Pete's sake, man, can't you tell one bloody car from the other? Can't you identify the different makes or colours?" he asked in the voice of a very frustrated man.

"I thought I was doing a pretty good job of that," I replied. "But I really don't pay that much attention to whose car it is when the red flag's up. To me, corp, a violator is a violator and those penny-pinchers have got to learn to take the penny out of their pockets and drop it in the meter. I sure don't want to be responsible for the town losing out on that penny."

"Forget the penny," he snapped. "Please, Adams, try a little harder. Please, for my sake and for your sake," he pleaded.

"I'll try, corp," I assured him.

It appeared that the good folks who parked on the streets of Humboldt were not used to the efforts of a conscientious young horse cop assigned to meter duty. I was going through a goodly number of tickets and by the end of the first week, I knew that I was going to surpass the previous year's total. By the second week of day shifts the number of tickets fell dramatically. That is, all but tickets on the mayor's car; they held steady. To the casual observer, it may well have appeared that I was following the mayor around town. He kept me busy writing and I kept him busy making regular trips to the detachment office with a collection of my latest efforts. This year's parking meter stats had a rocky ride. The detachment could have hit a new record that year if we could have counted the mayor's contribution. In spite of the numerous cancellations, the numbers continued to rise along with the corporal's frustration level.

By the third week, I became aware of more changes as I walked down the street with my ticket book in hand and my pen at the ready position. I observed some folks charging out of a building ahead of me and fumbling to feed the meter the required penny before I arrived. Ha! I thought. No one wants to part with a dollar, but they hate losing that penny even more. It was, to say the least, comical.

One day, I reversed the route I normally took. In doing so, I approached the stores from a different direction. I had to smile when I saw some folks peering down the street in the direction I usually came from. They were so intent on watching that they never saw me arrive. In some cases I would write the ticket, put the envelope on the windshield, then walk by, wave and point to the car.

But the mayor's car continued to be a target. It was always good for a little envelope. It was a sad day when the corp called me in. "Well Adams," he said, and I could sense that he spoke with a heavy heart. "I think it's time that we broadened your horizons a bit, son. I think you've mastered the art of writing meter tickets, so for now I want you to lay off the meters for awhile."

"Right, corp," I replied. I returned to my desk where I holstered my pen and I dropped the ticket book in the basket for a well deserved rest. I left the office for a little field trip on the streets of Humboldt. I never glanced at the meters once, except the violated one where the mayor's car was parked. The mental block was gone. I spotted that little baby from a block away.

THE ELECTRIC SPEED TIMER

"Adams!" The bellow from inside the walls of the private office resounded throughout the building and shook the outer office.

"Right here," I called back and leapt from my desk, my feet barely touching the floor as I charged into the corporal's office.

"I want a speed trap set up on Highway 20 south of town today," he growled.

"Hot dog," I replied. At last I was going to the field and I was going to be doing some real police work. "When do I start, corp?"

"You know how to run the timer, Adams?"

"No, I don't," I replied. "But I'm a fast learner."

"Oh yes, I'll just bet you are. Have you ever seen anyone run a timer?"

"Can't say as I have."

He gave me a funny little grin. "I'd be willing to bet a

month's wages that you've never even seen a timer, have you?"

"No, I can't say as I've ever seen one either, corp," I replied. My enthusiasm was dwindling as the conversation continued and I could see my field slipping away.

"Constable," he moaned. "Didn't they teach you anything in training?"

"Not about timers, corp, but I can march and ride a horse and if I do say so myself, I can sponge out a horse's dock with the best of them," I chuckled.

"Okay, I'll get someone to show you what to do then," he grumbled. "Go on and get ready to go out."

"Right," I answered, happy for the chance to get out of the hot stuffy RCMP detachment office above the post office in Humboldt, Saskatchewan and into the field. That directive sounded like music to my ears. Most of my field trips had been confined to shaking doorknobs every third week. My stint on the penny parking meters had lasted only slightly longer then my episode with the tear gas canister, but I had long since retrieved the book of tickets just in case I found a flagrant violation during my other duties. Although, since most of my field work was confined to the office, I had to admit that my chances of finding a car parked at a penny meter in the office were mighty slim. My career was charging right ahead as my training continued. I knew that before long I was going to be an expert in the finer aspects of police work. If the truth were known, I was probably ready to be working plainclothes right now. My forte was to be dealing with hardened criminals. But one step at a time for now, meet each challenge as it was presented, and I was ready for the next challenge. Bring on the timer, I smiled to myself.

I quickly learned that setting up the electric speed timer

was no simple task, for in addition to the timer, it required two men, one patrol car, complete with a certified speedometer, a hundred-foot tape, one ticket book, a reliable ballpoint pen and two empty wooden pop cases.

With the necessary equipment assembled, my mentor advised me there was one ingredient that could not be gathered in advance: A hiding place. Every speed trap requires a good hiding place, I was assured on the drive toward the south end of town. "There can be no successful speed trap unless you have a good hiding place." Obviously, I was with one of the best for I was shown the perfect spot to hide, a small patch of willows on the east side of the highway. "You have to be on the right-hand side of the highway in order to get people coming into town," my mentor advised me.

"What about those folks leaving town?" I asked. "Don't they ever speed?"

"Oh yeah, all the time, but we don't worry about them," he laughed. "They're usually going like a bat out of hell and they're tough to catch. You don't want to try to flag them down."

I was really enjoying myself on this fine afternoon. There was no doubt that field work really agreed with me. I was born to do field work, I thought as I helped set up the electric speed timer for the first time. But my mentor was an old pro at setting up the timer. He wasted little time in getting things moving and expended no energy. He barked orders and I did what I was told. I stretched two wires across the highway. We measured the distance between them with the one-hundred-foot tape. I got to hold the end that started with 1". My teacher was down tape from me, where the numbers were, I presumed, somewhat bigger. When he was satisfied, I assumed that the two wires were the required distance apart. The wires were then hooked to the electric timer box, which in turn was set on the observation deck, the top of one of the pop cases that he had instructed me to set on end and conceal in the willows.

With the trap set, one constable, me, took a perch atop the second pop case, which was sitting on its side, right behind the timer where I could easily read it. From my perch, I looked around and surveyed the countryside. Now I could see why we didn't waste time on catching cars coming from town. Drivers coming from the south could not see me in the willows, but to those coming from the north I sat out like a beacon. Sitting on the pop case, I peered through the willows, watching for oncoming traffic. While I carefully settled in, my mentor, the other constable, took the patrol car south along Highway 20. The signs advertising the town of Humboldt and its speed limit disappeared behind the cloud of dust. When he returned, I couldn't see the sign that read HUMBOLDT, in fact, I couldn't see the sign that read SPEED LIMIT 25. I never even saw the patrol car returning until it appeared through the dust just before the first speed trap wire. Instantly, I found myself sitting in a cloud of dust as he drove over the two wires. Somewhere down the road, he spun a U-turn and returned. He stopped the car and kicked up more dust before he waved me over to the car. Grudgingly I trundled through the settling dust over to the side of the car. "How fast was I going?" he called through the closed window.

"Sorry, I can't hear you, you'll have to roll down the window," I hollered back and held my hand to my ear.

"How fast was I going?" he yelled quite a bit louder. He was not about to let the dust in.

I shrugged my shoulders to indicate that I couldn't make out what he was saying. Grudgingly he rolled the window down just a bit. He tilted his head up and yelled again, "How fast was I going?"

"How fast? Oh, well the little box said fifty," I replied.

"Right on," he replied proudly. "Check me again." The tires spun, kicking up rocks and dust as he roared away for the second run. This process was repeated several times, insuring the reading on the timer corresponded to that on the speedometer of the patrol car. When the speeds had been confirmed and I was covered in dust, he declared that the trap had been properly set.

After the final run, I voiced my objection to the final phase of setting up the perfect electric-timed speed trap. However, it was once again pointed out to me that I was after all not only the junior member on site, but the junior member on staff. Recognising my place in the hierarchy, I grudgingly proceeded to the next task on the field trip. Walking out to the centre of the highway, I began to kick gravel over the two wires. The spit shine on my boots, the one that had taken a good thirty minutes to perfect, was already dulled by the dust. It completely disappeared in about thirty seconds as I kicked and pushed the gravel over the wire. When I had finished kicking, where there had once been two black wires there were now two little rows of gravel spanning the width of the highway. The speed trap was complete.

"Think you can handle it now that I done everything for ya?" yelled my mentor after I had finished covering the wires and returned to the willow blind to keep my keen eye on the timer.

"Yeah, it's no big deal," I answered with all the confidence in the world.

"Good," he smiled. "I'll be back later, sometime before dark, to pick you up."

"What do you mean, you'll be back sometime before dark?" I asked. I jumped up and raced to the car, where he was still sitting. I couldn't believe that he was going to abandon me out on the prairie, alone and on foot. "What am I supposed to do with a speeder who decides to drive away instead of stopping?"

"Well, you could always try waving," he laughed. "And don't forget you're representing the force out here. You make sure that you're presentable when you stop anyone and you wear your hat at all times." Then he waved and drove away, leaving me standing in the dust.

Heaven help the unsuspecting motorist who chose this day to drive into Humboldt from the south. The junior constable was on a field trip, alone, and he was manning the speed trap. He was covered in dust and was not what you would call a happy camper.

I sat on my perch, on my pop case, like a vulture hovering over a carcass as the cruiser disappeared. As the dust settled and the countryside took on the colours of a bright summer's day I started to feel good. Man, but it was exciting to be out doing actual field work. Out in the great outdoors, no phone, no typewriter, no paper. Criminals, that's what there were, criminals, and I was ready for them. While waiting for these doers of evil, I had plenty of action. I swatted flies and mosquitos, but mostly I fried under the hot prairie sun as I sat behind the willows. I peered through the leaves and twigs, searching the highway, looking for the poor unsuspecting soul who accidentally roared into my trap. Although not a part of my formal training that day, I quickly found that I had to make adjustments to my perch in order to get the best view of oncoming traffic.

The odd farm vehicle crawled by, well below the speed

limit, but I was well hidden, nobody saw me. Then, from way down the road, I heard a farm dog barking. I looked up and sure enough, there was a big old cloud of dust billowing skyward. "Aha," I chuckled. "Action." Finally, my patience was being rewarded. Business, announced by the barking dog, was on the horizon racing towards destiny. I braced myself in anticipation. "Baby, are you in for a surprise," I chuckled out loud.

My heart was racing when I realized that this sucker was really moving. Huge clouds of dust billowed up behind his car and he was making no attempt to slow down. Man, this is what I had been waiting for, real police work. The adrenalin was really pumping as I slipped off the pop case and crouched on the ground, ready to spring into action the second the timer registered a violator. I watched as the unsuspecting driver raced toward the trap. He did not know it, but he had a date with me and the local magistrate. I didn't wait for the tires to hit the first wire; if I was gonna stop this mother, I had to get out there and fast.

I figured those signs down the road had to look like a picket fence to this guy and I didn't need the timer to tell me what was happening. "SPEEDER!" yelled my brain and all my training and preparation for field work kicked in. My right hand shot up to my head and I smacked my Stetson down hard, setting in firmly on my skull. Then, my whole body uncoiled like a tightly wound spring. An RCMP officer, me, Constable Adams, in full uniform, sprang to his feet. I shot through the clump of willows like a wounded buffalo and bounded forward. I was a blur, my feet barely tickling the grass as I crossed the ditch and charged onto the edge of the highway. I was headed in the right direction. But before I got to my destination, the centre of the road in front of that speeding car, I began to have some serious second thoughts. "Whoa," yelled my brain as my boots hit the loose gravel and the car roared toward me. What if this maniac doesn't see me in time?

"Stop," I screamed. When it became apparent that the car still wasn't showing any sign of slowing down, I was sure the driver hadn't seen me and I began to backpedal and wave. I kicked up quite a little storm. Rocks and dust flew towards the centre of the road as my boots skidded on the gravel. Frantically, I flapped my arms like some idiot trying to take flight, something I wished that I could do right about then.

I breathed a sigh of relief when the brakes were suddenly applied. There was no screeching of tires, only dust, sand and rocks; a huge spray of dust, sand and rocks. The debris spewed forth in a storm as the vehicle instantly skidded on the loose gravel. Little missiles were suddenly flying in every direction. I could see a look of sheer terror on the driver's face. I knew he had seen me now, for his eyes were open wide, they looked like huge white marbles popping out of his face. His mouth was wide open and he seemed to be hollering as his vehicle bore down on me. I saw him spin the steering wheel to the left, desperately trying to turn the vehicle and avoid hitting me. This instant reaction on his part caused his vehicle to spin completely out of control. Suddenly, I was facing a much larger projectile. To me it was like watching in slow motion as the car turned. I clearly saw the grille disappear and the side of the car and doors come into view. They presented a far more formidable danger. Now it was the broad side of the car bearing down on me.

It didn't take a brain surgeon to know that this vehicle was not going to stop before it passed over the very spot where I stood. I quit flapping my arms and in one frantic movement I turned and dove for the ditch. The car continued to spin and was travelling backwards, spraying me with dust and gravel as it ploughed over the spot where I had been standing. I landed face-first in the ditch and threw my arms over my head. I lay there in a cloud of dust, afraid to move. I felt no pain and wondered if I was alive or dead. Then I realized that I felt no Stetson, either. My Stetson had not been set on my head as firmly as I thought. Somewhere between the road and the ditch I had dived out from under it. Then, I recognized a familiar noise. Somewhere in the distance, beyond my sight, out there in the settling cloud of dust, there was a motor running. No, on second thought, it was a motor roaring.

I gathered what was left of my confidence and extracted myself from the ditch. I searched around until I found my Stetson. It was lying on the highway, covered with dust and gravel. I knocked the crud off it as best I could, then with my hands I brushed the dirt and grass from my uniform. I carefully placed the dirty Stetson on my head, then, remembering my partner's parting words, I adjusted it to make sure that it was sitting properly. Now I was ready, properly attired, with all parts of my uniform in their proper places. All parts looked like I had been crawling in the ditch all day. Hesitantly, I picked my way forward, toward the sound of the engine. Through the haze, I could see the outline of a car. It was angled southwest on Highway 20 almost the same direction from which it came. It had come to a stop quite a distance past me and the willow patch. The driver was still in his seat, both hands on the steering wheel and he looked positively stunned, staring straight ahead. Well, actually, if he could see through the dust, he was staring into a field of wheat and beyond, into the broad expanses of the Saskatchewan prairie, the site of my first real field assignment. He looked like he had just seen a ghost. It was several minutes before he attempted to speak.

"Hi," I greeted him. "How are you today, sir?"

"Holy shit!" he stammered shakily when his voice returned. "I don't believe this."

"Are you okay, sir?" I asked.

"I'm not sure," he replied as he peered through the dust, looking around the countryside that was finally coming into view. "Did...you see that?"

"What's that, sir?" I asked.

"That idiot who jumped out on the road in front of me. Did you see him?" he stammered. "Oh man, I think I hit him," he moaned.

"I don't see anybody," I replied, looking back through the settling dust. In the haze, I could see the two pop cases stuck in the clump of willows. "There's nobody laying on the road," I replied. "And I just checked the ditches. There's nobody lying in them, either."

"Are you sure? Oh man, I hope you're right. I hope I didn't kill somebody," he stated.

"Oh, yeah, I'm positive," I assured him. "You might have come close, but you didn't kill anybody."

"Where'd you come from anyway?" he asked as though he suddenly realized that I was there.

I looked down at what had once been a clean pressed pair of pants with a yellow stripe running down both legs. The pants and the stripe were now both the colour of dirt and my shirt looked like a reject from the rag bag. "I was just out for a little field trip," I smiled through my dust-covered face. "Tell me, my friend, don't you think you were going a little fast?"

"Yeah, I guess maybe I was," he mumbled. "You sure I didn't kill somebody back there?"

"No, you didn't kill anybody, but you came pretty darn close. Now I would suggest that you slow this thing down a notch or two. Think you can do that?"

"Yeah, I guess so," he replied and then took a long look back down the road from where he came.

"You have a good day, sir, and a safe trip now," I said and waved him on his way.

He took one more look down the highway, then shook his head and drove away. I watched as he drove his car very slowly into Humboldt. Then I slunk back into my hiding place, the perfect speed trap. Sitting there in the willows waiting for the next vehicle, I had ample time to reflect on my field trip.

I reassessed my situation and future as an electronically timed speed trap *horse cop*. I decided there was really no future.

Suddenly my thoughts were interrupted by the barking dog, followed by the sound of another speeding vehicle. Another unsuspecting soul was charging towards Humboldt. Once more I peered through the willow blind and observed the cloud of dust approaching. As the tires hit the first wire, I tried to raise my right hand, to leap from my pop case, but my internal spring that had been so tightly coiled earlier in the day had not been rewound. From atop my perch on the empty pop case, I waved unseen at the driver as he flew past my post, spraying me with dust and gravel. I picked up the timer and the two boxes. I moved further into the clump of willows.

The mosquitos seemed to be hungrier in the centre of the willow patch. I swatted one and became aware of a lump in my shirt pocket. I reached in and retrieved a book of one-dollar meter tickets. Maybe, I thought, just maybe being a meter Mountie wasn't all that bad.

As I nestled back into the willow blind clutching the ticket book, in the distance I heard the farm dog bark yet again. I could just picture that dog laying in the ditch and charging out to greet every speeding car. I had often seen dogs like that. Obviously there were two of us on that highway looking for speeders. I decided that there weren't enough speeding cars to go around. The dog could have my share. I sat and waited for my pick-up to arrive. My first field trip had been a real barn-burner. Lucky to be alive, I sat in my perfect speed trap hiding place. I swatted flies and mosquitos. But mostly, I ate a lot of dust.

BABY DUCKS

Somewhere along the line, in my short tenure on the force, I had learned to economise. Unless it was absolutely necessary, I avoided driving the cruiser aimlessly up and down main street, burning up my precious five-miles-per-night shift allotment. If I banked even one mile a night, then if the opportunity arose for a drive in the country, I could get out just a little bit further. This bit of economy certainly had its benefits, especially for a young fellow who yearned for field trips. Every once in a while, on a beautiful spring morning when the sun rose long before the inhabitants of town, I would seize the opportunity to use the banked miles and take an extended trip into the quiet countryside.

The graveyard shift had been uneventful. In fact, it had been a very peaceful shift. So peaceful was it that I had taken the cruiser and made an extended patrol out of town. There are few places that are as beautiful and peaceful as the prairies on a sunny spring morning, I thought as I parked the cruiser on a country trail near the edge of a small slough and watched the sun rise. I watched the white-tailed deer peacefully grazing near a patch of willows on the far side of the pond. Meadow larks were singing from their perches on top of weathered fence posts. The surface of the pond seemed to be alive with ducks, hundreds of newly hatched ducklings, little balls of yellow-and-black fluff that would scoot across the water like little motorboats when they strayed too far from mom.

The whole earth was at peace with itself on this morning. Not a cloud could be seen and the dew sparkled like diamonds in the first rays of the morning sun. The air was so clean and pure and it smelled of the freshness of spring. This was one field trip that I wished could go on forever. I did not relish the thought of returning to town, but all good things must come to an end. I turned around and slowly drove back into town.

When I crossed the tracks, I noticed a strange vehicle with a large low trailer parked in front of Sam's Café. It was parallel-parked in an angle-parking zone and taking up four penny meters, a no-no in Humboldt. On the deserted streets this unusual unit stood out like a sore thumb. It hadn't been anywhere in sight when I finished my rounds and started my field trip just before daybreak. It warranted a look-see.

As I pulled along beside the trailer, I noted the Louisiana licence plates and was somewhat surprised to see Florida plates on the station wagon. I parked in front of the vehicle and got out of the patrol car. I was immediately greeted by a chorus of yapping, snarling dogs. They were kennelled in the trailer and they sounded mad and hungry. I think they were of the impression that I might well be breakfast.

I walked around the unit and made a few mental notes. There were a half-a-dozen dogs in the trailer and as I walked by, they commenced to howling loud enough to wake the dead. This was a brand-new ball game for me. I had never encountered anything like this in all my travels.

There were only two customers in the café when I walked in. I noted that they were two rather large male customers and they were enjoying themselves, laughing and joking as they ate bacon and eggs. They paid me no mind as I walked in and approached their booth. I could tell immediately that these two were cool dudes.

"Morning, gents," I addressed them as I stopped at their table.

They stopped talking and looked up as if seeing me for the first time. "Good morning, officer," they both said it almost simultaneously with a heavy southern drawl. Then, as best as they could in a booth, both attempted to stand up and offered their hands. "Join us for breakfast," one of them offered. Then, without me having to ask any further questions, they volunteered that they were agents with the US Fish and Wildlife Service, Don and Chuck. I was green with envy as I listened to them tell me that as a sort of reward for outstanding service they had been given the opportunity to band ducks in Canada's duck factory. They had jumped at the chance to come north to enjoy Canada and breathe some of that good, pure, fresh prairie air. As luck would have it, they had been assigned to this area of Saskatchewan for the spring and summer.

"Tell me, guys, how do I go about getting a job like yours?" I asked, sliding onto a seat in the booth. These two guys were being paid to do what I had to sneak out of town for just a peek at. "I'd love to be able to spend the summer banding ducks."

They both laughed. "Now don't you go thinking it's all peaches and cream, boy," Chuck drawled. "It's not as easy as it looks. We git ourselves into some pretty sticky situations at times. We don't always come out smelling like a rose." They both chuckled again.

"Yeah, well I'll trade a pile of paper and a year's supply of graveyard shifts for just a little of that smell, roses or otherwise," I replied. They both laughed and waved it off. "I take it that those are your dogs out there?" I asked.

"You bet they are," replied Don. "Them's the best bird dogs that money can buy. We been using them up here every summer for the past...oh, I don't know, three, four, maybe five years now, I guess."

"You mean you been coming up here banding ducks for that many years?" I asked, hardly able to believe my ears. How could anyone get a plum like this? One year seemed to be out of the question, but three, four or five years in a row, that was incomprehensible.

"Well, not right here," answered Chuck. "But up here in Canada. We do cover some of the same ground, but we work it so we get to see some new country every trip."

This sounded absolutely incredible to me. Two fellows were being paid to spend the summer in Canada and all they had to do was band ducks. "I take it then that Humboldt is new country for both of you?"

"Well, not really, we passed through here a couple of times now. Y'all sure do have nice duck country around here," Chuck commented.

"I suppose we do," I replied. "I never really thought of it before. But now that you mention it, yeah, I would have to say we do. You know, I've never banded any ducks before. For that matter I've never even seen a banded bird. I wouldn't mind seeing you fellas in action some time. That's if it's all right with you."

"Don't see why not. Once we get established and get things working, we'll give y'all a call and y'all can come out with us on your day off," offered Don. "How does that sound?"

"Oh, it sounds great, but we don't get too many days off in this detachment," I grumbled.

"Come on now," he laughed. "Y'all git days off, hell, boy, everybody gets days off, even 'horse cops'." They both roared at the joke.

"Okay. Let's take a look at my schedule and see what my days off are. How long you fellas gonna be here?"

"We'll be around here about a month I guess, give or take a couple of weeks," Chuck offered.

"In this detachment, a day off is considered a twenty-four-hour period. That comes between the afternoon shift which ends on a Saturday at midnight and graveyard shift that starts on Sunday at midnight. My first day off in the next three weeks is the third Sunday from now. Off at midnight Saturday and back on again at midnight Sunday. I don't suppose you boys work Sundays?" I asked.

"Sundays!" Chuck answered and looked positively horrified. "Don't y'all know that's a day of rest, boy? No way, we sure don't work on no Sundays."

"Yeah right, you're game wardens and you don't work Sundays? Tell me another one."

"What he means is, we don't work no Sundays when we're on these banding trips," Don laughed. "Are you sure you're levelling with us now?" he asked and gave me a funny little look. "You know, I talked to a horse cop up here a couple of years ago and he told me that y'all got one day a week off."

"Not me," I replied. "The best I can do is one Sunday every three weeks."

"Well, don't y'all worry none, young feller," Chuck

assured me in a very serious tone. "We'll get y'all out and band you some baby ducks. Even if you don't like ducks, y'all will really enjoy the day."

"Hey, that sounds great," I replied enthusiastically. I could feel a real field trip shaping up. "Tell me, how do you go about catching these little guys? Like I said, I've never even seen a banded bird in my life. Do you set up traps or what?"

"Well, you can use traps all right, that's certainly one way to do it," replied Don. "But we use the dogs, they pick up the birds for us and we band 'em. We try to keep it nice and clean. Using traps and fences can get to be an awful lot of work. A fella can get himself dirty and smelly wrestling all that gear around in the mud on the edge of a slough. We quit playing in the dirt years ago. We really don't like to get dirty, if you know what I mean." We all laughed.

"So..." I asked looking from one to the other. "How do you catch them little ducks?"

"With the dogs," Chuck replied. "Like we said, them dogs outside there, they're bird dogs. We use the dogs. They catch the ducks for us."

"Sure they do," I laughed. "You want me to believe that ducks are dumb enough to let the dogs walk up and catch them just like that? Those dogs that thought I looked like breakfast when I walked by them? They're going to pick up baby ducks and bring them back to you alive? I don't think so," I snorted, letting them know I thought they were pulling my leg.

They both looked at each other and had a good laugh. I could see their minds working and their looks seemed to say, "Boy, have we got us a live one here".

"No. No," Don said when he finally quit laughing. "The young birds can't fly yet and the older birds are going through

160

their moult, it's a stage where they lose all their flight feathers. Just like the little ducks, they can't fly either. You see son, the birds are always out in the middle of the ponds when y'all arrive but as soon as you all walk up to the edge of the water, they swim to the far shore and take cover in the grass. We let the dogs loose and they work the edge of the water and the grass. As they find the birds they pick them up and bring them back to us. We put bands on them and record their age and sex and then release them again."

"And these dogs, they catch these birds alive and then bring them back to you and they're still alive when you get them?" I knew what the dogs at home on the farm would have done to any bird they picked up, dead or alive. There wouldn't have been enough of that duck left to put in a bag, let alone put a band on it. Now I was sure they were trying to put one over on me.

"Look, son." It was Chuck's turn to try to convince me. "These dogs are specially trained to find ducks and bring them back to us, alive. They're the best dogs money can buy. They never harm a feather, they have real tender mouths."

"Yeah, sure," I laughed. "When I walked by those tender-mouthed babies, I saw their fangs and they weren't made of rubber. I had a chance to look into their mouths, they were teeth right back to their butts. Those ivories were made for biting and chewing, not soothing feathers on a terrified duck."

They both laughed. I'm sure they couldn't believe that they had found someone so devoid of knowledge about the capabilities of hunting dogs as the young horse cop sitting across from them at the breakfast table.

"Y'all gotta believe me now," Chuck said in as serious a voice as he could muster. "These dogs will not harm one feather on any of the birds they pick up. They're trained to do this and that's all they do. If one of them gets to the point where a bird gets hurt, he's off the team. Y'all can go to the bank on that."

"Sure, sure," I replied. I wasn't believing much of what they were saying.

"I think it would be better if y'all could see for yourself just what we do and how we do it. We'll make it a point to get y'all out even if it's just for a half day." They were just about killing themselves with laughter at this point. I had a good idea what they were thinking as they got ready to leave.

"So where you boys heading for now?" I asked. I really didn't want to lose track of the opportunity to get out into the field for a day. I didn't really care whether the dogs ate the ducks or not. "You fellas wouldn't be looking for some ducks to band today, would you?"

"We'll see. We'll probably just have us a little look around and if we get attacked by some ducks with a leg in the air, we'll stick a band on 'em," replied Don. "But first we intend to look around and see what there is for water. We haven't spent much time in this particular area before."

"Well, maybe I can be of some help to you then," I offered. "I saw a lot of mallards with young on a small slough earlier this morning. In fact, they're just a short way out of town if you're interested."

They both stopped and looked at each other. Now I had their attention. "You bet. Just point us in the right direction. If there's any baby mallards there, we'll git 'em."

I borrowed one of Sam's napkins and drew them a map of the area. I pinpointed the slough and I pointed them in the right direction.

I left Chuck and Don talking at the front of their vehicle, and I walked back for one more look at the cotton-mouthed dogs. The dogs again showed me their teeth and I knew that they were not the tender-mouthed mutts they were purported to be.

"Do you think he knows what a mallard is?" I heard Don ask Chuck.

"He's a nice enough boy all right, but I'm not even sure he knows what a duck is," Chuck replied.

"What d'ya think, should we go have a look?"

"Why not, it can't hurt anything. Can it?"

"I guess not," Don replied.

I stood and watched the two doubters as they climbed into the vehicle and started off on their duck banding expedition. One day I, too, would be able to control my field trips, I thought as I returned to the detachment office and signed off.

Actually signing off was a very loose term as the single men's barracks, three bedrooms, were located across the hall from the office. Right handy, just in case someone needed anything or there was an emergency. Help was always close at hand. I flopped down on my bed to get a few winks. I could hear the corp talking on the phone and the clack, clack, clack as someone pounded on the old Underwood typewriter. I rolled over and with these sounds ringing in my ears I fell asleep and I dreamed.

I dreamed that I was on a field trip. I was with Chuck and Don and I was on my way to band ducks. I was riding along with them in their station wagon and the dog trailer was bouncing along behind as they drove down the trail to the edge of the prairie slough. Everything was exactly as I had described it. Don and Chuck were congratulating themselves on their good fortune, having found someone as astute as myself to help them find a jillion baby ducks.

"And to think I had some doubts. Why, I think I owe this

young man an apology. You sure knew what you was talking about," Don sang out. "Just lookit that slough! Man, this place is alive with ducklings. We can probably get a whole week's quota right here," he laughed.

Just like I had told them, there were ducks of many species, but the majority were mallards and pintails, the very birds they were after. I knew this was going to be a field trip to remember. We would be at this bonanza for most of the day. My find was beyond their fondest dreams.

"Can I help with anything?" I asked, eager to be involved.

"You just stand back and watch us pros. We'll tell you when there's something you can do," Don replied.

Chuck busied himself getting the banding equipment out of the station wagon while Don got the dogs out of the kennels. Meanwhile I busied myself watching the ducklings move to the far side of the slough. They were rapidly disappearing into the reeds and grass. But Chuck and Don were unconcerned; everything was working like clockwork. It was a perfect spring day in a perfect world. What more could a duck bander ask?

Don released the dogs and they took off racing straight for the slough. Don and Chuck were right, them dogs knew exactly what they were doing. They didn't waste any time searching the grass and reeds on the near side of the slough. Not finding one single little duck, they charged through the water, heading for the far shore where the ducklings disappeared.

"Well young fella, you may not be too smart when it comes to banding," Chuck said. "But I have to give the devil his due, you sure knew where to find the ducks."

"You can say that again," Don whistled as he prepared for the rush and the hundreds of ducklings that would soon be dropped at his feet.

The dogs entered the water and were splashing around in the long grass and reeds looking for ducklings. They were working their way to the far side when a strange thing happened. Out of nowhere, right in the middle of my dream, the corporal appeared. He hadn't come out with us, but there he was standing right there beside Chuck and Don. "Ooowheee!" he exclaimed. "Something stinks like shit in here."

Back on the slough, the first dog had picked up a little duck and was making his way back to the banding crew. Other dogs followed behind and sure enough they had little ducklings and those babies were being carried in mouths as soft as cotton. The first dog arrived with his little prize. "Go ahead, young fella," Don said to me. "Y'all can take that one from the dog now."

I was just reaching over to get the little duck when the corporal appeared again, right in the middle of the banding crew. Suddenly, Don and Chuck were cursing and shouting at the corporal. Then I heard the corporal's voice, loud and clear. "Now calm down," he roared, then with a smile added "Man, do you guys stink." The corporal was right, I thought, there does seem to be a faint odour. Then I woke up. Oh man, the corporal had not been exaggerating. There was a putrid smell. It had crept under the door and had engulfed my tiny bedroom, choking me. It was enough to knock a skunk off a gut wagon and I heard the corporal say, "Boys, I'm sure Constable Adams didn't realize it was the sewage lagoon."

HOBO

Hobo? I distinctly heard the corporal say hobo. The word caught my attention, and I became much more aware of the conversation. I cocked my ear in the direction of the corporal's office. I did not want to miss a word, for I had long had a fascination for hobos and their lifestyle.

"I see...I see...okay, there's just one hobo then...right...I see. Now, you're sure there's only one? Okay then," the corporal said, speaking into the telephone. "I'll have an officer drop by and check it out immediately. Thank you for calling." Since I was the only officer in the detachment office other than the corporal, I quickly deduced that I would be the officer checking it out. I grabbed my Stetson, walked over to the key rack and removed the keys to the cruiser. I was up and ready for action, the hobo patrol, as the corporal exited his office. "Adams, I want you to go down to the station," he stated. "Apparently, a hobo jumped off the last freight train."

"You called on the right guy, corp. Constable Adams, hobo patrol specialist, is rarin' to go. But I always thought that hobos jumped onto freight trains," I chuckled, recalling some of the stories my dad had told me and all the old cowboy songs I had heard over the years. "You know, corp, all them old cowboys, they always sing about hobos 'just awaitin' for the train'," I yodelled. "There was never any song about them jumping off."

"Well smart guy, this one has jumped off," he mumbled, obviously not too impressed with my knowledge of hobos. He must have noticed that I had the car keys in my hand. "No. No, Adams," he moaned as he walked over to me. He reached out and gently removed the keys. "I don't think you need the car. The station's only a block away and besides, look outside, son, the sun's shining, it's a nice day. I think the walk just might do you some good."

"Whatever you say, corp," I replied, thinking that running down a hobo would be a welcome change from my regular town duties. "Anything in particular you'd like me to do with this hobo...if I find him, that is." The very thought of trying to find the hobo brought back some very vivid memories, memories of my father's stories about riding the rails in the hungry 30's and memories of the hobo jungle at Edson.

I could just picture my father regaling us with stories about trying to find work in the dirty 30's. He would often be sitting in the living room slowly pickin' on his old guitar as he talked. "Let me tell you about a time when Grandfather John and I rode the rails," Dad had often said. "We were living in Turner Valley at the time and jobs were scarce. Grandfather somehow got wind of some jobs comin' up in the Wildwood area, but we had to get ourselves up there. Now, we didn't have much money in those days and couldn't afford to by two tickets on the bus or train.

"How much money you got, boy?" Grandfather asked Dad that night at the supper table.

Dad dug deep into his pockets and dropped every cent he had on the table. Grandfather hauled his money out of his pocket and plunked it down with Dad's. Then he very carefully counted it. "Hell boy," Grandfather declared. "There ain't hardly enough money here to buy a decent meal, let alone two tickets. But you're in luck, boy, 'cause I'm gonna get you to Wildwood."

"How you gonna do that?" Dad asked.

"You ever rode the rails, boy?" Grandfather asked.

"Can't say as I have," Dad replied.

"Well, I have and I'm gonna show you how it's done," Grandfather stated as he scooped all Dad's money off the table. "We leave in the mornin'. I'll have you in Wildwood by nightfall," Grandfather tooted confidently.

Just like Grandfather promised, Dad said, Grandfather showed him how it was done and the two of them jumped the train to Edmonton.

"Wasn't it dangerous?" someone would ask. "Oh, yes," Dad would reply, shaking his head. "It was dangerous, all right. We really had to keep our eyes peeled for the 'bulls'."

"Were they real bulls?"

"No," Dad would chuckle. "They were policemen who worked for the railroad and their job was to keep the hobos off the trains. The bulls were always patrolling the tracks when a train was leaving town and if they caught you...."

"Were you scared of the bulls, Dad?"

"I sure was," Dad would reply. "They were big and mean and if they caught you, they'd either bust your head open or throw you in jail. Sometimes they'd do both."

"Wow!"

"Your Grandfather and I made it to Edmonton and had spent the day hiding back from the tracks, but we had us a good spot where we could see everything. We didn't want to miss the train. We didn't see hardly another soul while we was waitin' for dusk and a slow-moving freight train."

"Why were you waitin' for dusk?"

"So we could get a little closer to the tracks without the bulls seeing us," he replied. "It had been a while since we had eaten. My belly was growlin' up a storm as Grandfather and I waited. Grandfather said we should wait to eat until we got to Wildwood. Dusk came and went and it was blacker than the inside of a cow before a freight train finally rolled down them tracks. As soon as the engine passed us I could see men. They were all around us and all moving towards the tracks. There were hundreds of them. They seemed to jump right up out of the ground. As the train started to pick up steam, everyone started to run. I tell you, it was like a stampede. I could hear them puffin' and blowin' as they raced in the darkness. Some must have fallen because there was sure a lot of scrambling in the gravel and cursin' goin' on."

"What did you do, Dad?"

"I got to figurin' that if I didn't make my move, I was goin' to be trampled or worse yet, there would be no room left on that train. I jumped up and ran with everyone else. I lucked out, just as I got to the tracks I found me a flatcar that was rolling by. I got a hold of it and was able to get aboard and lay me down so's the bulls wouldn't see me. There was already a bunch of men on that flatcar and I got stepped on plenty as more scrambled aboard."

169

"Where was Grandfather?"

"Well, once I jumped up and started runnin' I never saw or heard from him. But as soon as we hit the country, I called out for him, but he didn't answer. It was a long train and I figured he must have been on another car. It wasn't the smartest thing I did when I jumped on that flatcar. It was a cold frosty evening and I just about froze to death. Every man on that flatcar huddled together like a bunch of rats tryin' to keep warm. I was one cold and hungry miserable man when that train finally slowed down near Wildwood and I bailed off that train. It was a good thing there was no 'bulls' there, my legs were so stiff and sore I could barely walk to the bush. But I hustled away as quick as I could. I figured I'd been pretty lucky in avoiding the bulls so far and I didn't want to get caught now. There were already a few boys in the bush when I got there. There were little fires burning all over the place. Some of the boys were boiling up a pot of tea. Others were huddled right over the flames trying to keep warm. One guy took pity on me and offered me a place at his fire and gave me some of his tea. When I warmed up a bit, I walked from fire to fire looking for Grandfather, but I couldn't find him in the dark."

"Where was he?"

"Well," Dad chuckled as he picked another chord. "I waited until morning and then I checked the bush again, but I couldn't find him anywhere, so I wandered into town. By now, my belly was really complainin' and I figured Grandfather had to be as hungry as I was so I checked out the station and the restaurants. But I couldn't find him anywhere in town. I met every freight train that rolled through town that day and each time I expected to see him bail off and head for the timber, but he never came."

"Did Grandfather ever come?"

"Oh yes, he came all right," Dad laughed. "That night, I was cold and hungry enough to eat the hind leg off of a horse when I saw the bus pull into town. On a whim, I thought maybe I should check it out. Sure enough, when the bus stopped, the first person off was Grandfather and he was grinnin' from ear to ear."

"Am I glad to see you, boy!" Grandfather had greeted me. "I lost you when everybody started runnin'. I tell you boy, I was worried sick about you. I didn't know if you could make it onto that train without me. Then I got to thinking that if you made it, boy, you were gonna need me and I didn't want to waste any more time gettin' out here, so I decided it would be better if I grabbed the bus."

"Where'd you spend the night?" Dad asked Grandfather.

"Jail," Grandfather replied. "Can you believe it, boy, I spent the night in jail with about twenty other guys. There was hardly enough room to lay down. Then this mornin', they kicked us out without givin' us any breakfast. Can you imagine that, I didn't get any breakfast this mornin'."

"Why did Grandfather spend the night in jail?" someone would ask.

"Well, as Grandfather told the story, he jumped the train all right, but then a big bull got a hold of him and yanked him off. Yes, Grandfather, the man who was goin' to show me the ropes, got busted by the bulls and had spent the night in jail."

We always liked to ask the next question. "What did you have for supper?"

"Well now, let me see," Dad would say as he slowly picked the guitar and his eyes got that faraway look. "What did I have for supper? Hmmm. As I recall...Grandfather explained that he used part of our poke to buy his bus ticket. Then, while he waited for the bus, he was sitting next to the café. Because they hadn't fed him in jail and with the smell of the café food, he was real hungry, so he used most of the money that remained to buy his supper. But he had saved enough to buy some tea. That night, we shared our tea with some of the boys in the jungle who didn't have as much as we did."

Dad could always find the humour in that story and I loved to hear it. It was one of the few that Grandfather did not share with us. But for all the funny stories, there was also a serious side to his days of riding the rails. While most of the men who rode the rails were honest men looking for work, there were some that had obviously put the fear of God into my father. These men still rode the rails and lived in hobo jungles. As kids, we were cautioned about going in or near the place known as the hobo jungle. The hobo jungle was a large densely treed area, mostly willows that lay along the north side of the railway tracks just east of the CN station in Edson. As kids, we had two routes to choose from to walk home from school. One was east along the highway, the other, the shortcut, was to walk straight south from the school on 49th to the railway tracks. The last block on the east side of the road before the tracks was a heavily wooded area called the hobo jungle. There were lots of trails from both the road and the railway tracks leading into the hobo jungle. The trails were well-worn, packed down from constant use. Whenever we chose to go home via the shortcut, past the station and the Beanery, we had to walk, or rather run, past hobo jungle. The hobo jungle was a place that we all feared. No one knew for sure what or who lived in the hobo jungle, although there were many stories around about the men who rode the rails.

They were a bloodthirsty lot and it was a well-known fact, confirmed by anyone who could talk, that the hobos only came out to jump a train or to steal. From the stories that I had been told, I was certain that when a hobo was not on a train or in the hobo jungle, he was running. Running to catch a train. Running into the hobo jungle. Running out of the hobo jungle. And with the exception of my Dad, hobos were probably running to steal something, or running from stealing something. Yes, hobos were runners, probably they were born runners.

Now, I knew for a fact that this hobo, the unfortunate one who had chosen Humboldt as his dropping-off place, had a problem. For, as anyone who had ever been to Humboldt knew, there were no trees and therefore no hobo jungle around the Humboldt railroad station. When I pictured the scene around the station, I knew that there was nowhere for a hobo to hide. Humboldt did, however, have miles and miles of open spaces. This hobo, I chuckled to myself, had better be one fast skinny runner, for he was going to have to run like the wind if he was going to get away. Of course there was an option. If he was skinny enough, he could always crawl on his belly like a snake and hide in a stubble field.

"Well corp," I chuckled, thinking that I may have to run him down and crack him on the head with my riding crop. "Tell me, what would you like me to do with this hobo when I catch him? Book him?"

"You buy him a meal, then put him on the next train outta town," he said without batting an eye.

"Buy him a meal? Now that's a noble cause, but I don't think so," I countered, laughing at his joke. "I'm broke."

"Nobody's asking you to spend your money, Adams," he replied.

But the corporal wasn't joking. He was dead serious. "I don't understand," I replied. "It doesn't make sense to me. Since when did we start buying meals for hobos?"

"Since I said so. Besides, he's hungry and he's probably broke. Now get on down there and pick him up. Take him to Sam's Café and feed him," he ordered. "Charge the meal to the town and bring the receipt back here. When he's finished eating, then you take him back to the station and put him on the next train out of town. Now, that's quite simple, isn't it? That shouldn't be too hard for you to understand."

"Yeah, simple enough, but I still don't understand, why are we buying a hobo a meal? It doesn't make sense," I protested. "That's not what we were taught in training. If someone's broke and hanging around, they're a vagrant. I thought that if you did anything with them, you busted them for vagrancy, or cracked them over the head and ran them out of town."

"Well, this is not training and you'll do this because I said so," he stated, raising his voice several octaves. It reminded me of a sergeant-major on a parade square. "Now move it."

"Okay, okay," I replied, somewhat hesitant as I moved to take on my latest assignment. But as I wandered down main street and thought about it, I started to have second thoughts about my earlier misgivings and wanting to crack this guy on the bean. I kept getting this picture in my mind. This guy was no longer just a hobo. I could picture my father in his place. I could see it now, somewhere, this man had a wife and probably children. They were waiting at home, hoping that he would be able to find work, hoping that he would send home enough money to buy a small amount of food. This was an opportunity to meet a man who was now going where my father had been. A man down on his luck, hoping to stave off starvation. It was a chance for me to help a fellow man in need. "Yes," I muttered out loud. This was certainly a job to my liking.

There was just one little hitch. Where would I begin my search? Where would a hobo try to run and hide in a place like Humboldt? My eyes were searching the horizon, looking for the vanishing form of the fleeing hobo as I walked around the side of the station.

"Well, you certainly took your time getting here," grumbled the man sitting on the bench at the front of the station.

"And a jolly good day to you, too," I greeted him. I was feeling pretty good with my latest assignment and wasn't about to let anyone pee on my parade. "Isn't it a nice day for a walk?" I asked and walked by without waiting for an answer. Obviously the grump had also seen the hobo and had expected a quicker response, I thought as I walked into the station. "I understand we've got us a hobo?" I greeted the station agent.

"We certainly do," he replied.

"Did you happen to see which way he ran?" I asked the station agent.

"He didn't run," replied the agent. "That's him sitting out there on the bench at the front of the station."

"That's the hobo?" I asked, walking over to the window and looking out at the grump. "You're kidding me, right?"

"That's him all right. I saw him jump off the freight myself. Then he walked over here to the station and sat down on the bench like he owned the place. You better get him out of here. I don't want him hanging around."

"You're sure?" I questioned him again, then took another look at the guy on the bench. "He don't look like no hobo to me."

"Well, he's a hobo all right. Now go on and get him away from my station before he steals me blind."

"Holy mackerel," I mumbled. "Hobos have certainly changed since my Dad's days of riding the rails."

"A lot of things have changed, son," replied the agent. "By the way, next freight's due through here around five this afternoon."

"Thanks," I replied and went back outside. I stopped in front of the bench and looked at the man sitting there. If this guy was down on his luck, it didn't show. He certainly wasn't my idea of a hobo, nor did he match the description of the hobos my father had often talked about. To me he looked like any ordinary guy, about average height and weight. If he had missed any meals, it certainly didn't show. He had a neatly trimmed beard. His hat was a fairly new fedora and he wore a pair of slacks, a shirt and even a sports coat. His ankle boots looked to be brand new. At his feet lay a rucksack that seemed to be fairly well packed. He looked like he could have been a business man waiting for a train. If I hadn't known better, this guy could have completely destroyed my image of a hobo.

"Well, have you seen enough? You satisfied now?" he asked again. "You know, a man could starve to death if he had to wait for you every day."

No, I thought, there must be some mistake, this guy did not look like a hobo and he certainly did not act or sound like a hobo. Then it dawned on me. I cursed myself for being so stupid, to be sucked in. Once again the rookie had just been duped. Another initiation. Someone had to be sitting back killing themselves laughing. "Who put you up to this?" I asked.

"I don't know what you're talking about," he replied. "I just came in from Yorkton."

"Sure you did," I grinned at him and took a seat beside him on the bench. I looked around expecting to see someone I knew standing back splitting a gut as the rookie tried to figure this one out. "Tell me, where are you really from and who set this up?"

"Originally I'm from back east," he stated. "And I have no idea what you're talking about. I just got off the train and I'm hungry. Now shall we go and get breakfast? You know, people around here won't be very happy with you if I miss the next train."

"Really," I chuckled. "Well, since the next train's not due until five, we've got a lot of time, haven't we? Now, suppose you tell me, how'd you really get here?"

"You must be new here," he smiled. "You fresh out of training?"

"Oh, I been here for a while now. You could say I'm almost a seasoned veteran. Why do you ask?"

"Because you sound like a rookie. You're as green as grass. Right out of Regina, I'd say," he chuckled. "Tell me, you from Regina, son?"

"Nope, not me," I smiled. "But I did spend a night there when I passed through. Like you, I'm from back east. Now, I'd really appreciate it if you'd tell me where you're from and how you got here?"

"Well, let's just say that you're a rookie and like I told you, I'm from back east and I came by train," he smiled. "I rode in on the last freight train."

"Well then, Mr. Hobo, how long you planning on staying in Humboldt?"

"Well, let me see now," he said, stroking his beard as he contemplated his answer. "If I was a betting man, I'd bet the good people around here don't want the likes of me hanging around on their streets. I'd say I'll be here long enough to get a good meal. After I eat, I'm sure that you'll convince me to leave on the next train."

"Passenger?" I asked.

"Freight," he replied quickly. "The price of a ticket on the passenger train is a bit steep for me."

"Right," I answered. "I should have known better."

"Are we going to go up to that old Chinaman's café now so's I can get something to eat?" he asked.

"That's right. Sam's Café. How'd you know that if you just got into town?"

"Oh, I've been here before and that old boy serves up one of the best breakfasts on this route. I wouldn't miss it for anything."

"Okay, let's go and get it over with then," I replied and we walked around the side of the station. My vision of a true hobo was quickly vanishing as this conversation progressed.

"Where's your car?" he asked, looking around at the empty street. "I don't see your car."

"I didn't bring the car," I replied. "Like I said before, it's a nice day so I decided to walk."

"I never had to walk before," he complained.

"Well, if you want breakfast, you're gonna haveta walk this time," I stated as the two of us shuffled off up the street to Sam's Café.

"What you want?" asked Sam as we took a booth near the back of the restaurant. Sam was a man of few words.

"Tell me Sam, what kind of a meal does the town buy for hobos?" I inquired before ordering.

"You pay," asked Sam, looking at me.

"Not me," I replied. "The town's paying, Sam. The good people of Humboldt, Saskatchewan are setting this man up

178

today. Unless you want to buy his breakfast."

Sam turned and looked at the old clock on the end wall. "Bacon and eggs," he replied.

"Don't forget the toast and coffee," the hobo interjected quickly. "I get toast and coffee, too."

"Toast and coffee too," Sam confirmed the oversight.

"And you," Sam looked at me.

"I'll have a glass of water," I replied.

"You want a coffee?" Sam asked.

"Water's fine."

"I'll bring you a coffee. You no pay."

"Sam," I replied, looking up at him. "Every morning I come in here for breakfast and every morning I have toast and a glass of water. I don't drink coffee, remember?"

"Okay. Bacon and eggs. Toast and coffee and one glass water," Sam replied and turned away.

"Don't hurry with the breakfast," the hobo called after Sam. "My train doesn't leave until late this afternoon."

"Tell me," I said returning my attention to the hobo now that the water issue had been resolved and Sam had an official 'slow' on the bacon and eggs. "What kind of work are you hoping to find out here in the west?"

"Work?" repeated the hobo like I had just hit him over the head with my riding crop.

"Yeah, work," I replied. "What kind of work are you looking for? I just assumed that you were riding the rails, looking for work."

"Work? Me work?" He was obviously shaken by my bold assumption. "Not me. No thank you, my young friend. I'm certainly not looking for any work. Why would I want to work?" he replied and sounded like he was genuinely upset. "Whatever gave you an idea like that?"

"I don't know," I replied, somewhat surprised at his answer. "I just thought that it was mostly people who were looking for work that rode the rails. I know my Dad used to tell me stories about riding the rails in the dirty 30's. There were hundreds of them and they were all looking for work. He said that was the only way they could travel because nobody had any money. I guess it was just this stupid idea I had that everyone wanted to work."

"Well, this is not the hungry 30's and I'm not one of the multitude that use train travel for that purpose," replied the hobo, sipping the hot coffee that Sam placed in front of him. "I'll have you know that I'm on a tour of Canada."

"No kidding," I said, realizing that my whole concept of the hobo was being dashed to pieces by this man. "That...does sound interesting. But, as I understand it, you have no money. How you gonna tour Canada with no money?"

"That's easy," he laughed. "You don't need a red cent, and you can see this country from coast to coast. Right now, I'm on my fourth trip out west."

"Your fourth trip!" I replied, not really believing my ears. "This is your fourth trip? You've got to be kidding me."

"Nope, I'm not kidding. I've been to every part of this country, well, every part that the trains run to, that is. I guess I've seen every city from Halifax to Vancouver several times now. You know there's a lot of trains running through Canada."

"Get outta here," I replied, shaking my head. "You're pulling my leg, right? You've got no money and you're riding the rails. You really want me to believe that you've been across Canada four times?"

"You don't need any money to ride the rails," he said quite matter-of-factly. "And after the first trip, you get to know where the good hand-outs are at."

"You mean, like breakfast right here in Humboldt."

"Absolutely, why... why I wouldn't think of taking a trip out west and not stopping at the Chinaman's café in Humboldt for bacon and eggs."

I took a sip of my water and suddenly it tasted very much like alkali. "Sam," I called out, "did you get this water out of the tap?"

"No. It's bottle water," Sam replied.

"It tastes of alkali," I complained.

"Maybe taste from dishwater," Sam chuckled at his little joke.

"I never drink the water in these little prairie towns," the hobo confided to me in a very serious tone.

"Why not?"

"Too much alkali in the water. Gives you the screaming meemies something fierce," he replied and nodded his head. The hobo was obviously a man of great experience. His breakfast arrived.

"I don't suppose you've ever been sorry that you never went to school and then got a job?" I asked, trying to figure out a man who was obviously content to tour the country and feed off of others, a parasite.

"Everything isn't always as it appears, you know. I have been to school and I have had a couple of jobs," he said, looking past me, probably into his past and some distant memories. "I taught school for a few years when I was back east, then I worked at a couple of office jobs. You may not believe it, but I do have a degree, you know."

"No, I didn't know. Why would anyone want to quit and ride the rails if he had all that education?" I asked.

"I really wanted to travel," he replied. "And I couldn't

make enough money. In fact, I could barely make ends meet."

"So, you just quit."

"That's right. I woke up one morning and decided I'd had enough. The next day I found myself on a flatcar heading west. Would you believe it was colder than hell and I didn't know enough to get into a boxcar? But a man learns fast when he's alone and on the road. You quickly learn where to sleep and where to find a hot meal. That's why I'm here right now having this fine breakfast and enjoying your company."

Later in the afternoon, as the hobo trotted out towards the slow-moving freight train, I watched how casually he flipped his rucksack onto a flatcar then nimbly leapt aboard. He stood up and waved goodby. I stood on the platform and watched until the train had pulled out of sight. As it disappeared into a warm prairie afternoon, it left me with a sadness that I had never before known. I could not help but feel for my father and the many thousands of men who rode the rails trying to eke out a living from a very unforgiving land. Now, less then twenty-five years later, this man, this hobo, was riding the rails, doing well living off of hard-working decent people's fear.

"You know, corp," I said when I returned to the office and told him the story. "When you first told me to go pick him up, I sort of resented it, but then I thought about it and what I was doing. Man, I was on the top of the world when I picked him up. It's hard to explain how good it was to be helping a man in need. You don't know how proud I felt to be a policeman at that moment. But by the time I left him, I had a different feeling. I really think I would have felt better if I had busted him over the head with my riding crop."

"Well, that's police work, lad," replied the corporal. "Some days it's good and other days...well, there are a lot of other days. You just have to learn to put them behind you."

"Yeah, I know, but there's got to be something wrong with this picture. Here I am working six days a week, 10 to 12-hour shifts keeping this town safe. I shake doorknobs at night for the good businessmen of this town and I write dollar tickets for penny meters. Hell, corp, I've even been known to jump out of willow patches in front of speeding cars. I pay for my own breakfast at Sam's Café, toast and a glass of water because that's all I can afford. I've been nowhere, in fact I'm saving every penny so that I can go home to my sister's wedding. And this hobo, who tells me he's been across Canada four times now, rides in here on the rails as big as life and I have to go to the station and meet him and bring him to Sam's Café and the town buys him bacon and eggs for breakfast. You know, corp, I have to ask myself, who's the idiot in this little scenario?"

"Have you found the answer yet?" he asked.

"Yeah, I think so, and I can tell you I sure don't like the answer I keep getting."

"Tell me, Adams," the corporal asked seriously. "Were there any break-ins in town today?"

"Not that I know of," I replied.

"Well, I can tell you that there weren't. Now, do you think that guy will commit any crimes in our town tonight?" he asked.

"I doubt it."

"Well constable, then I haveta say you did one hell of a job of crime prevention today. You should be proud of yourself."

"When you put it that way, I guess I have to admit to just a tinge of pride," I replied. "However, corp, remember that hobo is now on his way, he's gettin' a free ride to Saskatoon and I'll bet you a month's wages that he knows exactly where to go for a free supper tonight. Say, corp, since I did such a good job today, do you think the town fathers would pay for my supper tonight?"

"They probably won't, but I could be talked into it...if you promise to jump the next freight and follow that hobo out of town."

THE SILENT BURGLAR ALARM

The sudden, eardrum-piercing noise erupted without any advance notice. The first CLANG! certainly got my attention and scared the living wits right out of me. I just about broke both my legs in my haste to get out from behind the desk and dive for cover.

It was a hot sunny prairie afternoon in Humboldt, Saskatchewan and there were two of us on duty in the RCMP detachment office. It was one of those prairie days that one could best describe as stifling. The air conditioning for the office amounted to opening the windows and letting the hot air pour in. It was debatable which was hotter, the air outside or the air inside. Just sitting at the desk and lifting one's eyelids was enough activity to cause streams of perspiration to flow off one's brow. I hadn't moved far from my typewriter all day, moving only the tips of my fingers, and my shirt was soaking wet.

I have to admit that I was a wee bit lethargic, maybe almost comatose, certainly only a step or two from sleep when the inside of the office was jolted by this horrible clanging noise. I, the newest member and the rookie on detachment, had never heard this piercing, pulsating noise before. I had never heard anything like it before in my life. It was hard on my ears and it scared the dickens out of me. In my hasty exit from my desk, I had succeeded in scattering the contents on my desk all over the floor. I managed to catch the typewriter before it followed the paper and basket down. I glanced quickly around the office to locate the source, to see who or what had decided to liven up our day, but there was nothing to be seen. The sound that filled the office seemed to be coming from nowhere and everywhere. Now, I may have lacked experience, but with my keen sense of self-preservation, I knew immediately that it was something serious. "What the hell is that?" I yelled over the nauseating sound.

My partner, who had considerably more experience then I, knew immediately what it was. "Bank robbers!" he yelled loud enough to be heard in the next town. He immediately leapt to his feet. I noticed that his desk was left intact as he rapidly vacated his seat and bolted for the walk-in vault. "Somebody's hitting the Bank of Nova Scotia."

"Where?" I asked, still looking around the room for the noise.

"Across the street," he yelled back at me. "C'mon. Don't just stand there, follow me."

"How do you know that?" I shouted back at him and stepped back over to the south-facing windows. If I had stayed in my chair behind the desk, I could have just turned my head and looked out the window. From there, I had the best seat in the house. The Bank of Nova Scotia was located right across the street and I could look right down on it. In fact, I could see right through their windows. I could even see the tellers behind the counter. I could see that the bank employees all appeared to be sitting in their chairs quite calmly going about their duties. In fact, everybody had their heads down and appeared to be working as if nothing at all was happening. They, of course, were oblivious to the howling alarm that was wreaking havoc with my eardrums.

"It's their silent burglar alarm," my partner bellowed above the screeching. "Nobody knows they've set it off except us. This is the only place where it rings, right up here in our office, nowhere else," he yelled again as he spun the dial frantically. Obviously my partner had decided that it would be in our best interests to have something in our hands, preferably our revolvers, when we responded to the call.

"Right on," I replied. A bank robbery, and on my shift, too. Finally, there was some real police work. This was what I had been waiting for. Today, I would be catching some real criminals. Man, but this was exciting. I didn't have a clue what I was doing, but it was exciting all the same. I raced over to the vault to assist my partner in retrieving our weapons.

Our revolvers, yes, that would be a good idea. If we were going to have to shoot somebody, then we would definitely need our revolvers. But first we had to get them and that was what he was trying to do. The revolvers, along with the ammunition, were safely stored in the large walk-in vault. The vault, I was told, was a remnant from a bank that many years ago had occupied the building. The vault, like the building, was older than dirt and rocks and sometimes had a mind of its own.

Now, getting that door on the old vault to open was no easy task at the best of times, but with the secret burglar alarm blaring and the adrenalin pumping, the combination to the door suddenly became very elusive. My partner cussed like a trooper and sweat poured off his brow and down his face. My partner was soaking wet and the closest we'd come to responding to the complaint was the dial on the vault. He spun the combination again and again, then cursed some more, but the combination refused to accept the code. "Ever notice how combinations never seem to come together when you're in a hurry?" I shouted in his ear. I noticed that the dial resembled a spinning top.

He ignored my knowledgeable observation and cursed as he spun the dial again. It took several attempts before the tumblers dropped into place and the big heavy door finally swung open. The silent burglar alarm was still blaring as we raced into the vast interior. I followed my partner, the senior member on duty, and when he dropped to his knees, I dropped to mine. We were not praying, it was merely to begin the struggle anew, for the revolvers were not only in the walk-in vault, they were secured in a smaller safe. Once again I watched as my partner immediately resumed his struggle, this time with the combination on the smaller safe. As he spun the knob, I thought of my handgun stowed safely in the little safe and my mind flashed back to my firearms training.

On the day my troop was first introduced to the range and received their initial instructions, there was a void, one member was missing, me. As I had drawn other duties, I had to wait for another day before seeing any action. Sadly, I had missed the great event and my pistol had remained holstered. I hated to miss anything new and I waited with nervous anticipation as the next firearms training session approached.

I fretted about what I had missed. How far behind my troop mates would I be, I wondered?

But, I needn't have concerned myself, for the very next time we were scheduled for pistol training, I was there and I received my just dues. Only half the troop was in attendance on my first day at the range.

My troop mates with firing range experience marched over to the training hall. I marched along with them, I certainly didn't lack training in the marching department. Then in single file, we made our way down the single flight of narrow stairs to the range. I hadn't missed much here, for I could go down basement stairs to a firing range with the best of them. The RCMP recruit training range was very much like the army cadet range I had spent many hours at in Edson. It was located in the basement under one of the training rooms. In Edson, we had been under the bowling alley. One by one my troop mates made their way to the little set of benches at the rear of the range. This was better than the basement of the bowling alley. There I had to sit in the dirt behind the firing line waiting for my turn to shoot.

It was a small, dingy, musty place. Cobwebs appeared to be the only decoration in the very small quarters. No wonder only half the troop took firearms training at a time, we barely fit on the little benches. From my seat, I got a good look at the floor joists overhead. They showed the tell tale scars of many an errant bullet.

Then, after we were all seated and I presume it was because I had been absent the first day of firearms training, I was called to the front of the group. There, while my troop mates watched, I strutted out to the front of the group and received personal instructions on the proper way to handle a handgun. I was shown how to load a six-shot revolver. "You will only put five cartridges in the cylinder," the instructor stated. "Do you know why?" he asked.

"No, constable," I replied, wondering why I was issued with a six-shooter if I was only allowed to use five bullets.

"Why do we only put five cartridges in the cylinder?" he asked the troop.

"For safety, constable," they called out in unison.

"For safety purposes, Mr. Adams. Do you understand?" I didn't want to sound like a dummy, but five bullets in a six-shooter didn't make any sense to me. "I'm afraid not, constable," I answered.

"I didn't expect you would," he sighed as if this was another in a long line of hopeless situations. "Why do we only put five cartridges in the cylinder?" he asked the troop again.

"So you don't shoot yourself in the leg, constable," came the rehearsed reply.

"So you don't shoot yourself in the leg. Now do you understand, Mr. Adams?"

"Yes constable," I replied. But I had to admit, I wondered why anyone would be stupid enough to shoot themselves in the leg.

"Have you ever loaded a revolver before, Mr. Adams?"

"No, constable."

"Come here and let me show you how." Together we took about two steps to the firing line. There he took my handgun and flipped the cylinder open. He took five bullets out of a box and held them in his fist then slowly opened his fingers. In his palm lay five shiny cartridges. "How many cartridges are there in my hand, Mr. Adams?" he asked.

"Five, constable," I responded.

"Very good," he smiled. "And how many you will put in your revolver?"

"Five, constable," I replied again.

Very slowly and deliberately, he dropped one cartridge at a time in an empty chamber in the cylinder. When all five cartridges were in, there was one empty chamber in the cylinder. He closed the cylinder taking care to insure the empty chamber was under the hammer. I had to admit, I couldn't shoot myself in the leg if there was no bullet under the hammer.

"Have you ever fired a handgun before?" he asked.

I hesitated before answering, thinking of all the times in the barracks when I was cleaning the revolver and the many imaginary targets I had lined up in my sights and had taken imaginary shots at. But that was only dry firing, there were no bullets in the revolver. I didn't expect that dry firing would count, and if it did, it shouldn't. "Never, constable," I responded.

"Okay," he replied and popped the cylinder open then flipped the revolver towards the ceiling. Five shiny cartridges fell out into the palm of his hand. He flicked the handgun to the side, the cylinder closed and he handed it to me. "Now Mr. Adams, do you see that pile of targets over there?" he asked and pointed to a stack of targets that had the silhouette of a man on them. "Well, I want you to pick out one that you like and take it to the far end of the range and pin it up."

I walked over and checked out the targets. "They're all the same," I informed him.

"I know," he replied, shaking his head. "Just take one and pin it up."

Back at the firing line, I stood and watched the target I had hung up. It was so close. Although I had never fired a handgun before, I knew a man of my many talents was going to blast the thing to smithereens. I eagerly waited for him to hand me five bullets so I could commence shooting. I was going to stick one bullet in on top of the other. That target was calling to me.

Man, but you could have knocked me over with a feather when he handed me one bullet. "Only one bullet," I muttered. "I thought I was supposed to put five bullets in at a time... constable?"

"One will be lots for a now," he assured me. "Go ahead, take your shot so we can get on with it."

I felt like a fool, standing in front of my troop mates sticking one measly little bullet into the cylinder. Carefully, I stuck the cartridge into an empty chamber and closed the cylinder making sure it would rotate into the barrel when the hammer was pulled back. Then, knowing that the eyes of my troop mates were on me, I stood up straight, lined up the target at the end of the range, pulled back the hammer, aimed and squeezed the trigger. The explosion echoed throughout the basement and little wisps of dust drifted down from the rafters overhead. My ears were ringing. I thought I heard someone talking.

"Go get your target," I heard the constable's voice above the ringing in my ears. He was yelling at me but his voice seemed to be a long way off.

"Oh, yeah, right," I mumbled. I holstered my revolver and raced down the range.

"Well, where'd you hit it?" he asked when I brought the target back with me.

I took a quick glance at my target and then back down the range. Surely I must have taken the wrong target, but there was not another target down there. I spoke as softly as I could so the rest of the troop wouldn't hear. "I think I musta missed." I searched all over the target for any kind of hole, but except for the outline of the man and the circles in the chest area, the target was clean.

"Take a seat and see if you can learn anything from watching the rest of the troop," he said and motioned me toward my troop mates. "And take the target with you. At the rate you shoot, it'll probably last you forever," he laughed. I tucked my tail between my legs and crept back to my seat on the bench. To a country boy, who grew up with a twenty-two in his hands, with extensive experience firing twenty-twos and rifles in army cadets, I was used to shooting several rounds at pine-cones high up in a tree or at the eye of a cautious squirrel. Firearms training in Rockcliffe had not been what I had imagined it would be. I watched as the next recruit was called forward, the procedure was repeated. He returned to the bench after firing his shot, and his target was as clean as mine. It appeared that I hadn't missed too much the first day.

My first experience with the revolver had been a humbling one. I hadn't fired a shot since training, but the silent burglar alarm was blaring and I was ready for whatever lay ahead. Finally the door on the second safe clicked and my partner flung it open. He grabbed a Sam Browne and thrust it at me. "This one yours?" he asked, handing me a Sam Browne which contained a holstered pistol.

"Nope, that's not mine," I replied.

"How about this one?"

"Yeah, that's it," I mumbled. I took the belt and removed the pistol. There was no time to waste and certainly not enough time to strap on the leather, and I dropped my Sam Browne to the floor. With our revolvers clutched in our hot little hands, we both turned and raced out of the door. But we didn't get very far. Actually, we were barely out the door when my partner put on the brakes and stopped short. I was right on his tail and literally ran right up his back. "You got any ammo?" he yelled at me.

"No," I replied. In the excitement of the moment, I had forgotten that we always unloaded our firearms before we stored them.

"Well, we're gonna need ammo," he yelled. He spun on a dime and ducked past me and raced back into the vault. In our haste, we had both forgotten that for an added measure of safety, we didn't store the ammunition with revolvers. I turned and raced after him, back into the vault to retrieve the ammunition. I was beginning to get a headache. It had to be from that bloody alarm, which continued to blare.

Finally, we were ready and on our way again. In one hot sweaty hand, I clutched my revolver. By now the grip was just like me: covered in sweat. It felt hot and slimy. In the other hand I clutched the ammunition. The bullets felt as though I had retrieved them from a barrel of oil. They were so slippery, I knew I'd be lucky to get them into the cylinder without dropping them.

My heart was beating frantically and my body sweating profusely. It was, to say the least, one hot, sweaty, sticky day as I prepared to meet my first real challenge. Out of the office we raced, down the stairs, two, three, four steps at a time we bounded, then literally flew through the door. Without a word being spoken, I raced across the street toward the corner of the bank and main street.

While racing toward potential disaster, I was desperately trying to cram five greasy rounds into the flopping cylinder of my .38 Special. Although the cylinders hold six bullets, I, like every other recruit, had been trained to put in only five rounds and keep the hammer on the empty chamber for safety purposes. I remembered my instructions well as I charged across the street, in full view of the bank, I might add. No, the training had not been wasted on me. Here I was in a crisis situation and may have needed every shot, but like a well designed and trained robot, I put in the approved number of rounds: five.

I have no idea why, but I was headed for the front door. After all, that was the logical door to enter or exit a bank from. At least, I had never entered a bank in any other way.

Upon reaching the front, I suddenly realized that the front of the door was glass and any robber could easily see me. I stopped short of the front door. My partner, who had matched me step for step, was also at the front door. He too stopped short of the glassed front door. He motioned for me to take up a position on the far side.

"No way," I replied. "I'm not walking out in front of that door."

"Take the other side," he directed. "That's an order."

It was only about thirty inches across that opening, but man, it looked like a mile. Getting shot crossing a doorway wasn't really what I had in mind when I wanted to do real police work. I felt that I could do a lot better with the face-to-face stuff. I grumbled a lot and did not really feel like the cream of the crop as I braced myself for the quick dash to the far side. My legs seemed to be like mush as I crouched down. As I sprang forward, I prayed that it would not be my last act. Man, but I hated being the junior man on detachment.

I felt a little better when I realized that I had made the crossing and had not been shot. In fact, I had not even been shot at. I straightened up and even managed a weak smile. Standing out in the hot afternoon sun, I suddenly realized it really was a hot day. My knees were knocking and my whole body was trembling like a leaf. I was sweating like a hog. The water was literally running off my body. My shirt was soaking wet and I felt like I could hardly hold the revolver in my sweaty hand.

I looked across the space, the width of the door, at my partner. He appeared to be as cool as a cucumber, although the wet stains on his shirt told a different story. He was all business as he motioned for me to try the door. "Oh, sure," I mumbled. "The junior man gets to do all the fun things. No way," I protested. "Whaddaya think, I want to get shot?" I looked at the door, then back at him. "Try it yourself," I whispered so that the robbers inside the bank could hear.

"Try the door," he ordered and motioned me forward.

"But the knob is on your side." I pointed out the obvious oversight on his part. "You're closer to it than me."

"I told you to try the door," he ordered. "I'll cover you."

"Yeah, thanks for nothing," I mumbled. I plastered my body tight up against the wall and slowly reached out, exposing my left arm to the bandits inside. I knew if they had a shotgun, they'd blow my whole arm away. With my thumb and one finger I grasped the door knob. Like everything else on this miserable day, it too felt hot and sweaty. I turned the knob very slowly so as not to make any noise. But it wasn't the knob that was turning, it was only my thumb and finger sliding around the polished metal. I cursed, silently, then I gripped the knob with my whole hand and twisted harder, trying again. "The bloody thing's locked," I whispered across to him and quickly retrieved my arm.

"It can't be," he replied. "It's the middle of the afternoon."

"Well, it's locked," I assured him. "It won't turn."

"Let me try," he said and grabbed the knob and twisted. I noticed that his arm didn't have to stretch out across the door.

"It's locked," he confirmed. "I'll bet the robbers locked it."

"What do we do now?" I asked, and looked to the senior man for guidance.

"I'm not sure. What time is it?" he inquired.

"It's fifteen minutes past three," I whispered back, not knowing what difference the time would make.

"That's what I thought." He shook his head knowledgeably. "It's fifteen minutes past closing time. It's the ideal time for a bank robbery." Now, that comforting thought really got the blood pumping in my veins.

"We better go around the back and try the back door," said my partner, lifting his right hand into the air and pointing his revolver skyward as he turned around. At that moment, I distinctly heard the sound of metal hitting concrete. We both stopped dead in our tracks and looked down. My partner went white. There, rolling around on the sidewalk at his feet, were five .38 Special cartridges. We both looked at his revolver and saw immediately that in his rush he had not closed the cylinder. He was going to have to expose himself to retrieve all five cartridges. I waited and prayed that the robbers wouldn't choose that moment to come bursting through the door. My partner bent down and one by one he reached forward and retrieved each of his bullets. It only took a few seconds, but watching him, down on all fours collecting his bullets, exposed to the robbers, I could have sworn it was hours. As soon as he had the cartridges back in the revolver and the cylinder closed, it was time to move to the rear door. I jumped across the doorway and with my partner in the lead, we raced back across the front of the bank, down the side wall and around to the back door.

My partner was still leading the charge when we reached the door. To my surprise, and I'm sure to my partner's as well, the back door to the bank stood wide open. My partner and I continued our charge. Through the back door and into the back room we raced, heading for a second door that would take us into the main bank. I was hot on my partner's heels. As we charged forward I looked over my partner's shoulder and I could see the tellers. They were standing behind their cages, busily counting money, just like they were balancing out for the day. If that bank was being robbed, I thought, those tellers had to be the coolest folks on earth.

Suddenly my partner must have realized what we were doing for he slammed on the brakes and came to an abrupt halt. I didn't and I kept charging forward. I bowled into him and my momentum carried us both forward, until the two of us burst into the bank. Those poor souls had absolutely no idea that they were about to have more company. We were right there among the employees, among the tellers who were still labouring over the daily cash and receipts. Before those poor souls even knew they needed help, it had arrived.

My revolver was held out in front of me and I was combing the air, searching for the robbers. Actually, what I was doing was waving my revolver in the faces of tellers, for there were no robbers. At that point the bank staff came to the sudden conclusion that they were indeed being robbed. And to add to their horror, they were being robbed by two young Mounties. To say that we scared them out of ten years of growth would be an understatement.

"It's a robbery!" screeched the first teller that looked up and found herself staring into the business end of a .38.

"Don't shoot," yelled another and throughout the bank hands were instantly reaching for the ceiling.

"It's not a robbery," yelled my partner into the panic and confusion that we suddenly found ourselves surrounded by. "It's us. It's the RCMP. We're here to protect you."

"Please don't shoot me," wailed one poor teller, who started to cry.

My eyes searched the room, looking for an unfriendly hostile face, the real culprits. But there were no hostile faces to be seen. There was, however, fear and panic on every face before us.

"Your silent alarm went off back at the office," my partner explained to a somewhat bewildered manager who was shaking so bad that he couldn't speak. His lips moved, but not a single sound escaped.

No one could explain how or why the silent alarm had been tripped, but it had been, probably by accident. There had been no robbery in progress before we arrived, and the staff was grateful that one had not been committed when we left.

Back at the office, the silent alarm was still blaring, vibrating the entire building. My partner stopped in front of the door to the outside vault. "Adams, were you the last one in here?" he asked.

"I'm not sure," I replied. "I think I was the last one out the first time we left, but I'm not sure about the second time. Why?"

"Because you left the door to the vault open, you dummy. That's why," he snapped unhappily. "Now, you're gonna haveta check everything in here to make sure that nothing is missing."

"Why me?" I protested. "You were in here with me. In fact, you opened the doors."

"Then you should have closed them. You're the junior man around here," he replied.

As I settled down to my hot task in the vault, I thought about the events of the past few minutes. My first chance to realize my dream, to fight crime, to protect people, had come on a sweltering day in a prairie town. It had been a false alarm.

HE'S A DANGEROUS CRIMINAL, LAD!

It was the wee hours of the morning and the lights shining brightly in front of me were those of Davidson, Saskatchewan. As I stared at them, through the darkness, a cloud of dust swirled around the car and drifted toward the lights. Through the dust, the lights took on an eerie ghostly image, dancing before me on the open prairie. I clutched the steering wheel of the little red Volkswagen Beetle tightly in both hands and I shook my head as I tried to get my bearings.

"Adams, you horrible little man," I cursed myself loudly as the dust began to drift away and the dancing lights of Davidson cleared and once more shone brightly in front of me. "What on earth do you think you're doing?" I scolded myself as I looked around. In the darkness I could make out the flat summer fallow field where my Beetle had come to rest. "How in the hell did you ever end up here?"

I sat back to collect my thoughts and calm my shattered nerves. I could only shake my head at the chain of events that led up to my sitting in my almost new Volkswagen, out in the middle of some unknown farmer's summer fallow field in the early morning hours of a night in mid-September.

It was my sister's wedding. That's where it all started. At the time, my life was nothing but a series of highs. I had been home to Edson for her wedding and it had been a glorious affair. A Red Serge Wedding, right in my own hometown, and I had been one of the best men. Yes, I had been one of the lucky ones, and I had received permission from the force to wear my Red Serge. I was able to parade before my family and friends, one of Canada's finest, the cream of the crop, in my scarlet tunic.

After the wedding and a leisurely trip across Alberta and half of Saskatchewan, I returned to Humboldt in my brand spanking new red Volkswagen Beetle with my own bride-to-be sitting in the front seat beside me. Well, separated of course by the stick shift and the emergency brake, but for all intents and purposes, she was right beside me. There was no thought of us tying the knot in the foreseeable future as the force had a rule about marriage. We were going to have to wait for another three-and-a-half years before I met the required five years of service eligibility. But we considered ourselves lucky, for the five-year rule had just replaced the original seven-year wait. We were fully prepared to make the sacrifice.

Driving into Humboldt, in the late evening on that fateful day, I distinctly remember seeing a new member walking down main street. I did a second take, then chuckled as he hesitated, then tentatively reached out and shook a doorknob. There was no doubt that he was a rookie, maybe someone with a regimental number higher than mine. I wasted no time in wheeling the Beetle into the curb beside him, and chuckled again as he jumped. He was a rookie alright and I was sure he was the new junior member. Ah yes, this was my lucky day, I just knew I was getting up in the world. "I'd say you're new around here, aren't you?" I asked without introducing myself.

"Yeah, I am. Why?" he replied.

"No reason," I answered, feeling pretty smug. "How's it going?"

"It's going fine," he replied and gave me a look that was about as tentative as the one he had just given the door, then he cocked his head to one side. "Your name wouldn't happen to be Adams, would it?"

"It would at that," I replied, and bounced out of the car to shake his hand. "That's me. So, who you replacing?"

"If you're Adams, then I guess I'm replacing you," he deadpanned. "And by the way, I was told, 'If Adams shows up, and you see him, you tell him to call me immediately'. That's what the corporal said."

"Whaddaya mean me? Where am I going?" I sputtered. The smugness I had been feeling disappeared into the prairie evening.

"I have no idea," he replied, "but I do know that the minute you talk to the corporal, you're history in this town, man."

"You're kidding me, right?" I asked, unable to believe what I was hearing. I turned to look at my bride-to-be. I suddenly realized that by this time tomorrow, we would be in different towns, maybe even in different provinces. All of a sudden, three-and-a-half years seemed to be an awful long time.

"You can always stay and work on the farm," my bride-to-be chimed in. "Daddy's always looking for help, especially at harvest time."

"Now, you gotta be kidding me," I mumbled, thoughts of stooking grain and pitching bundles flashing through my head.

That part of the farm I didn't really have a problem with, but I saw the size of the rocks they picked in their fields. No thanks. Things were suddenly going from bad to worse. I didn't want to leave, but I sure didn't relish the thought of working on the farm for Daddy for the rest of my life, either.

"And I'm supposed to report to the corporal when?" I asked.

"As soon as I see you, I'm to tell you to report immediately," he assured me.

"Damn," I muttered, for I had a gut feeling that I may not spend another night in this little prairie town. "Tell me, my friend, have you seen me yet?" I asked the rookie rather meekly.

"Yeah," he replied. "Sure I can see you, you're standing right here in front of me." Then he laughed. "But I'll tell you what, if I happen to see this Adams guy the corporal's looking for, I'm gonna tell him to get in touch with the corporal lickety-split. If I was Adams, I think I'd go and enjoy my last night in town."

"Thanks," I replied. "See you tomorrow about noon."

"I don't think so," he answered. "I'll probably be asleep. Oh, and by the way, that room you used to sleep in, it's now my room. Please don't come charging in there tomorrow and wake me up. I packed your things into your trunk and had them hauled out. The corporal knows where they are."

At 1300 hours the next day, I learned that sometime during my absence, I had been transferred to Kindersley and was scheduled for the 1400 hours shift. "Where's Kindersley?" I asked.

"It's about 120 miles southwest of Saskatoon," the corporal replied. He just happened to have an old road map handy and he pointed to a spot near the Alberta border.

"There's Kindersley," he stated. "Right there. That's your new home."

"That's about two hundred miles from here! How am I going to get there for a 1400 hour shift?" I asked, looking at the corporal. "I can't even get to Saskatoon in one hour, let alone to Kindersley."

"Instead of standing here jawing, then, I'd suggest you get a wiggle on," he replied.

"I'll have to pack my stuff first," I replied, knowing that my packing had already been done for me.

"Don't worry about packing, lad," he responded. "Your replacement needed a place to sleep so I had him pack up things. I sent your trunk on to Kindersley for you. It's probably already there."

It was a little after five in the afternoon when I walked into the detachment office in Kindersley. The first person I met was my new corporal. "Can I help you?" he asked.

"I'm Adams," I replied. "I understand I'm your new man?"

"You're my new junior man," he answered.

"What else is new?" I mumbled.

"You are aware that your shift here started today at 1400 hours?"

"Right. I found that out at 1300 hours today."

He looked at his watch, then up at me. "Well, according to my watch, you have just enough time before your shift starts to grab a bite to eat, then one of the boys will show you around town."

"I was wondering," I asked. "You wouldn't by chance know the whereabouts of a wayward trunk, would you?"

"Don't worry about your trunk," he laughed. "It arrived, safe and sound. A couple of the boys are renting an apartment down the street. Your trunk's over there. They also hauled in an extra bed and set it up. I think you're more than welcome to stay with them and split the rent and groceries, if you want to."

"Sounds good to me," I replied. "How do I find this apartment?"

"C'mon, I'll show you. Oh, and by the way, welcome aboard, son. We're glad to have you here."

Kindersley was great. It was entirely different than working in Humboldt. I was really beginning to like Kindersley, but there were some things in my life that needed attention. I had some unfinished business back in Humboldt, bills to pay and accounts to settle, and it didn't take long before I noticed some definite changes. The biggee was the telephone bill. I just about died when I found out how much the long distance telephone calls were costing me. At the rate I was going, I would have to go on a patrol every day and stop at a farm house for something to eat. Otherwise, I was going to starve to death.

One day, I could wait no longer and I approached the corporal.

"Corp," I started to plead my case. "As you know, I had to pull up stakes in Humboldt on very short notice. I left a number of loose ends, you know, some strings untied back there, and some urgent unfinished business. I was wondering when it would be convenient to get a pass so I can go back and tie them up."

"What kind of strings?" he asked.

"Well, you know, corp, strings like ah...well for one thing, I've got some bills back there and they have to be paid. And there are some folks there that I got to know pretty well. It would nice if I could...like...well, you know, say goodby to them. I sorta did leave town in a hurry and after all, I don't want it to appear that I left town like a thief in the night."

"Make a list of who you owe and how much. We'll get one of the members to make payment for you. And you can write the rest a letter."

"You know, corp," I chuckled, thinking that he was kidding, "I would sorta like to straighten up my affairs with those folks...you know, like...face-to-face. And, well I've got a fiancé there, too, and I'd sorta like to see her at least once in the next three-and-a-half years before we can get married."

"Adams," he replied very sympathetically, "even if I wanted to give you a pass, which I don't, I can't. Furthermore, if your fiancé has any intentions of moving here, tell her to forget it. I can tell you right now, son, if she comes here, you're on the move again. I'm sorry, son, but that's the way it is. There'll be no pass. There'll be no girlfriend moving here. Now, I'd say that was pretty simple. Wouldn't you?" he asked, looking up at me. "Maybe you should consider tying up some loose ends in other ways."

Well, that little talk certainly took the wind out of my sails. "I'd say the whole thing's a crock of bull, wouldn't you, corp?" I replied.

"You could be right, son. I'll note that for future reference," he replied and dismissed me with a wave of his hand.

I had not been in Kindersley long, but it seemed like an eternity as the telephone bills mounted and the loose ends began to take their toll. Then one day, I received a telegram. Just like you see in the movies, rescue was on the way, and just in the nick of time, too. When I was with Forestry back in Alberta, I had inquired about a job as a game warden, but was told if I really wanted a job I should get some police training first. The telegram was from the powers-that-be from the

Alberta Fish and Wildlife Division, offering me the highly-sought-after position of Assistant Conservation Officer in Brooks, Alberta. Suddenly, there was a light at the end of the tunnel. This was the lever that would force the corp to give me a pass to go back to Humboldt. I could just picture the knots forming in those loose ends. Armed with the telegram, which I had tucked safely into my shirt pocket, I marched confidently into the corporal's office. "Corp," I demanded, "I've thought it over and I really want that pass to go back to Humboldt for a couple of days."

"I'm sorry, son," he replied. "Like I told you earlier, even if I wanted to, I can't do it."

"Then I guess I'll just have to purchase my discharge and go back on my own time," I informed him. I took the telegram out of my pocket and slowly and deliberately opened it. As he watched, once more I read the contents to myself. I looked up to see how my lever was working.

"Hold on now, son," cautioned the corporal, forgetting about the stack of paper on his desk. He carefully laid his pen on the stack and looked up at me. "Now, I think that's a pretty rash decision. After all, it's only a pass. Things like this have a habit of working out for the best. I'd suggest you just slow down and give it some time," he said in a fatherly way. "After all, this is a major decision. Have you really thought this through, son? Have you considered all the consequences?"

"I have, corp," I stated and for the third time slowly read the contents of the telegram. "I've got another job offer, back in Alberta. They tell me I won't need a pass to go anywhere and they'll even let me get married. I won't have to wait another three-and-a-half years."

"Just a minute, son. Not quite so fast," he cautioned me.

"Tell me if you've really thought this out. Have you considered everything, your future, what you're doing with your life?"

"I think I have, corp," I replied. "First thing I'm gonna do is accept this job. Then I'm gonna go back to Humboldt and tie up those loose ends once and for all. Then I'm gonna get married."

The corporal sat behind his desk, looking at me and the telegram. "Okay, then, if that's the way you want it," he sighed. He looked like he had just been whipped and I knew I had him. I was gonna get my pass. In a couple of days I would be back in Humboldt. You could have knocked me over with a feather when he added, "Since you're hell-bent on resigning, do you want your remaining time with us to be short and sweet or a long drawn-out and painful ordeal?"

"I beg your pardon?" I asked as the words seemed to have escaped me. This was not what I had planned on hearing. "What do you mean?"

"Do you want to get out of the force in a timely manner, or do you want to drag it on forever?" he asked.

I thought about the question for a minute. A few minutes ago, I had an ace in the hole, a real lever, and I really hadn't planned on getting out of the force, but I had called the shot and the corp had made the decision. Before I knew it, I was on my way out of the force and I hadn't got to do any real police work.

I had not actually given the thought of leaving the force that much serious consideration. But now my mind was racing as I tried to recall the stories told to me by others who had left the force before serving a full five-year term. Pictures were rapidly developing before my eyes; they were pictures that others had painted for me. An assortment of stories, all horror stories, flashed through my mind. But the one that kept recurring and that I could picture vividly was the member dressed in his fatigues carrying out his final assignments. The poor excuse for a human being, a brown gob, was crawling around on his hands and knees, clipping the grass in front of the subdivision office for over a month with a pair of small scissors. Pinking shears, if I recalled correctly. I cringed at the thought. "I guess short and sweet would be better," I stammered rather meekly. "Why?"

"Then short and sweet it will be. Sit down and let's make sure we word your resignation properly," he said and took out a fresh sheet of paper and started to write. "Let's see, now. Hmmmm," he paused, studying the paper very carefully. "Now, son, you say you have a girl friend, right?"

"Right, corp," I replied, taking a seat on the opposite side of the desk and watching him very deliberately pen the words that would decide my future.

"And, as I understand it, you're engaged, right?"

"Uh huh. Right. That's right again, corp."

"Well, as I see it then...I think maybe...maybe you really don't want to get out of the force. Maybe...maybe it's that you have to get out. Do you think that maybe that's really what you have to do?"

"If you think that gets me short and sweet, rather than scissors, then I think that...well, maybe that sounds fine with me, corp," I replied. "Short and sweet is what we're looking for here, right? As long as it's short and sweet."

"Believe me, son," he smiled. "This is short and sweet. I can guarantee you, you'll be outta here so fast it'll make your head spin."

"Right, corp," I replied. My head couldn't be spinning any faster then it was at that minute.

And short and sweet it was. In no time flat I received word that my presence would be required in Regina in about a weeks time to finalize my discharge. In the meantime I was to continue with assigned duties in Kindersley. Thanks to the corp and the carefully worded letter, nothing had changed. The horror stories were just that, stories. They belonged to others, not me.

However, it seemed that every day at the end of the shift I was asked if I would mind lending a hand, volunteering here and there to assist a fellow officer. I was just sort of the ride-along member, the second man in the vehicle. I'd just sit back and watch, but not be involved.

The first night there was a boring routine night patrol of the countryside. The only sign of life was the barking of a dog at every farmyard we cruised past. The patrol lasted until the wee hours of the morning. I figured I was lucky to arrive back in town in time to shave and report for duty.

The second night was a little better. A complaint from a small town in the detachment area stated that unknown persons, presumably from the bigger town of Kindersley, were using the town as a place to party. Further, the complaint continued, the rowdies were drinking in their cars, spinning U-turns on main street, just about the only street in town, and they sprayed gravel on everything in sight. The kids from the big town were terrorizing the locals.

A patrol was dispatched to deal with the problem. It was suggested that I might like to accompany the investigating constable. Now I was tired from the lack of sleep, but I was no dummy and about the same time it was being suggested, I remembered grass and pinking shears. I volunteered to ride along, as an observer of course. After all, I figured I could grab forty winks in the patrol car. Sometime before midnight, I was sitting half-asleep in the passenger's seat as the patrol car slowly prowled the street of the small town. "There's a car parked by the grain elevators," my partner whispered. "It's tucked back into the shadows. It's almost hidden from view."

"Uh huh," I mumbled as I sat up, took a quick look, then slumped back into the seat. The cruiser approached, slowly.

Suddenly the quiet was shattered by my partner screaming. "They're making a run for it."

"Where?" I yelled and sat bolt upright at the thought of a chase. I saw the headlights come on as the vehicle sped off into the night. The police patrol car answered the challenge. Wheels spun, spraying gravel around on the street when the patrol car fish-tailed before taking off like an arrow. The red light was immediately turned on, as was the siren. The whole town would know instantly that the law had arrived and on this night, justice was being served. If required in the future, I would be able to confirm we were indeed in hot pursuit after the departing car. With all the bells and whistles at our disposal working for us, it did not take long, only seconds, to race down the street, through town and into the country.

From my position in the passenger's seat, the second man along for the ride, I noted that we in the trailing vehicle were not in the most enviable position. We seemed to be eating an awful lot of dust. In the dark and the dust, I was able to observe very little of the countryside. Thankfully, the fleeing vehicle suddenly left the road and raced into a farmyard. The patrol vehicle skidded sideways and almost missed the approach, but I was in good hands, we stayed right on the tail of that culprit. It was good that we were now in the farmyard, I thought, noting that there was no dust where we were now driving. With the aid of the farm light I could plainly see the farm house as the cars raced past. Both cars spun and swerved around the barn, then headed back towards the house. The rows of vegetables stood up like sentinels for all to see just before the lead car hit the garden. The tops of the plants were mowed off like they had been cut with a scythe as the car fish-tailed and the tires spun in the soft loose soil. I was wide awake as the carrots, turnips and beets shot out from behind the spinning wheels like little coloured missiles, orange, purple and red. The wheels were still spinning wildly as the car bumped and bounced, then came to a halt on top of a row of monstrous cabbages. From my observer's seat, I was thankful that the driver of the cruiser was awake and alert, for he had to do some fancy driving himself to keep the tossed salad from running right up the back of the now stalled car.

I had been afforded very little sleep in the past couple of days, and by rights, I should have been dead tired. But I was not. Sitting in the middle of that garden, I was wide awake as I watched the participants get out of their vehicles and have a short discussion. The driver of the fleeing vehicle shrugged his shoulders and rolled his eyes, then he kicked the earth a couple of times as both men surveyed the scene. It was mostly dirt and assorted vegetables littering the ground.

I don't mind admitting that I was somewhat taken aback as one driver walked towards the barn and the other, my partner, returned to the patrol car. The one that went to the barn started up his tractor and pulled both vehicles out of his garden. "We're in his garden," was the only comment my partner made. In the headlights, I could see that a fair portion of the garden had been harvested, probably a little sooner than expected.

I was more than a little groggy, I was a whole lot tired as I neared the end of my shift on the third day. I was really looking forward to some badly needed shuteye. But the voice that seemed to be somewhere in the distance had a foreboding tone. My first thought was, where was I going on this night? "Adams, tell me my friend, have you ever transported a prisoner?" I was asked as my strenuous day shift rapidly drew to a close.

"Sure," I replied, sitting up in my chair. The question had sort of awakened me from a sitting slumber. Sitting up was more activity then I'd had all day. "Plenty of times. From the crime scene to the cells or to court."

"Well, am I ever glad to hear that," replied the constable who asked the question.

"Why?" I asked.

"Because I think you're just the man we need," he replied, slapping me on the back. "We have a real treat for a man with your vast talent and experience."

"What's that?" I asked.

"A prisoner escort," he chuckled. "You'll be pleased to know that you've been selected to take a prisoner to the pen at Prince Albert."

"Me?" I asked, somewhat taken aback. I was being asked to escort a prisoner, to do something out of the office and on my own. Man, here was the first real chance I had to do something that I thought was meaningful. "When?"

"Right now, as soon as you get the rest of your uniform on."

"Not me," I stated and laughed at the obvious joke. Wasn't that just my luck? Here I was, I hadn't slept in two days, I was dead tired at the end of another exceptionally long day and now I finally got a chance to do some real police work. "I'd love to, guys, but my shift's almost over for the day and anyways, I'm dead on my feet. I'm not volunteering for anything. In fact, I was just thinking it would be nice to go and slip into somethin' comfortable and have myself a nice cool one before I grab forty winks, if I can stay awake that long."

"Yeah. Right. I hear you loud and clear, *junior man*. But I'll say this much for you, you have got one helluva sense of humour, boy. Now, you may think you're out of this man's outfit, but you're not out yet, sonny," came the rather caustic response. This was followed by hilarious laughter from the rest of the boys in the room. "Look at this way," he smiled. "Why, it's a fabulous opportunity. It's an all-expenses-paid pleasure trip to beautiful downtown Prince Albert, Saskatchewan. Hell man, all you gotta do is sit back and relax." More laughter. "Now get a move on, hustle your butt and get into your full uniform. Oh, and by the way, do you still have your pistol?"

"Yeah, why?"

"Oh, I was just wondering, I was hoping they hadn't taken it away from you. Don't forget to take it with you. Now hurry, your train leaves in less than an hour and it won't wait for you."

It was like turning out for inspection. It seemed like everyone was there to make sure that I was properly attired for this onerous task. "Let's see now," said my tormentor as he slowly strutted around me. "I see boots, breeks, tunic, Stetson and Sam Browne. You got a pistol attached to that lanyard?" he asked, flipping the holster flap with his finger. "Oh yes, there it is. Now I see it," he smirked as he stuck his nose down close to the holster. "My goodness, constable, I am impressed, you even remembered your spurs. Come along then, I'll introduce you to your travelling companion," he said and handed me a file which contained the paper work.

My travelling companion, the prisoner, looked just like any ordinary man. He was about five ten, a hundred and seventy pounds. He didn't appear to be like me; on the surface he wasn't nervous, scared or excited. At the station, the prisoner stood beside me. He could have been just any other person from the farming community getting on the train. In full uniform, I was the only one who looked out of place.

"Now listen up, Adams," cautioned my colleague very seriously. "You keep your eyes on this guy at all times. He's a very dangerous criminal, lad. You be careful and watch yourself with him. I don't want to read about you in the paper, now."

I took a second look at the prisoner. He didn't appear to be any dangerous criminal, but then how does one really know? "Don't worry," I replied. "I haven't lost one yet."

"Not yet," he laughed. "But then, this is your first escort, isn't it?"

"Thanks a bunch," I mumbled. I turned and motioned to the prisoner to walk ahead of me toward one of the day cars, then halted him just before he was going to step on the conductor's little stool. I motioned for the conductor and he moved over beside me. "Apparently, I've got a real bad dude here," I spoke quietly to him. "You wouldn't happen to have a quiet secluded spot where we can be alone and I can keep an eye on him?"

"I don't know," he replied. "The train's pretty full. Wait here for a minute and I'll see what I can do." He stepped on the little stool, climbed the stairs and hurried into the car. He returned in a few minutes. "Follow me," he called from the top of the steps. "I've got two seats with your names on them."

I took one look at the two vacant seats and immediately thought he was kidding me. "Is this the best you can do?" I asked.

"That's it," he replied. "Unless you want him to sit at one

216

end of the car and you at the other."

I did not like these travel arrangements one little bit. Here I was guarding a dangerous criminal and I was going to have to share seats with a woman and a small boy. Our seats, mine and the dangerous criminal's, would be facing back in the direction from which the train was travelling. If he sat by the window, which is where I wanted him, then he was going to be sitting right next to my holster and my handgun. And I did not want him sitting next to the aisle where he could bolt away and I would have to give chase.

If this dude was really bad, then I wanted him sitting up against the window with me on the aisle, away from my sidearm. I'd just ask the lady to change seats with me. "How are you today, ma'am?" I asked in my friendliest voice. She had probably already guessed that she was going to have to share the seats with a dangerous criminal, and I did not want her to be too alarmed.

"I'm fine."

"I was wondering if you would consider changing seats with me and my friend?" I asked, hoping that she would not be scared out of her wits at the sight of this dangerous man.

"No, I would not," she replied. "We were here first and these are our seats."

Well, I thought, she's certainly not scared out of her wits. "Sorry, I was just asking," I replied and motioned to the prisoner to take his seat. Public enemy number one and I settled into our seats across from the lady and the young boy. The prisoner was up against the window. I was on the aisle. My trusty .38 Special Smith and Wesson revolver was tucked neatly into its holster right between the two of us. If this bird wants out of here, I thought, he'll have to go through me.

As the train pulled out of the station, I started to notice

that wearing my Stetson in the train was not very comfortable, so I took it off. I looked around to see where I could put it. In the crowded car, the options were limited. It appeared that I could set it on my lap, drop it on the floor, give it to the kid across the way or put it back on my head. I guess I should have looked for a place to store it before I took it off. I returned it to my head.

The young boy had not taken his eyes off me since I sat down. His mother, on the other hand, had not looked at me since I asked her to change seats. She sat and stared out the window. "How are you today?" I asked the little fellow and gave him a big old smile. He just sat and stared while his mother continued to look out the window. This had the makings of a long, silent train ride.

I turned my head and gave the dangerous criminal the once-over. He still appeared to be very calm. His face showed absolutely no emotion. He was looking straight ahead, like this train ride was just another everyday occurrence in his life. I looked beyond him through the window where I could see the fields of grain stretching beyond the horizon. Here and there a combine was chewing up the endless swathes of grain and the dust was hanging heavily in the air. The clickety-clack, clickety-clack, clickety-clack of the steel wheels on the tracks had a mesmerizing effect on me as I stared out on mile after mile of prairie.

My mind started to wander and my eyelids grew heavy. Then, I was back home, with my brother Larry. We were going fishing in the McLeod River at a spot known as the Big Eddy. But, instead of fishing, we had dared ourselves to walk out on the railway trestle, a huge wooden bridge that arched over a ravine. We were having a great time as we picked our way across the ties. "Don't look down, or you'll get dizzy and fall," I warned Larry as we gingerly stepped from one tie to the next, daring ourselves to go even further. We were right where a person didn't want to be if a train came, in the middle of the bridge, when we heard the shrill whistle. We turned and watched in terror as the big steam engine puffed its way around the corner and started over the bridge. I felt Larry tugging at my side as we raced to reach a small landing where track crews would sometimes pull a speeder off the tracks. But the clickety-clack, clickety-clack, clickety-clack of the wheels on the tracks was getting louder. We ran harder, faster in a losing battle. The engine was gaining on us, then the whistle sounded another long shrill blast. The ground seemed to be miles away, the clickety-clack of the wheels and the whistle right on top of us. Larry tugged at my side again as we prepared to leap off the tracks, over the side of the trestle.

Then I woke up in a cold sweat. The clickety-clack, clickety-clack of the wheels was still there, but getting slower. The whistle shrilled once more and Larry tugged on my arm again. I suddenly realized it was not Larry and we were not bailing off the side of the Big Eddy bridge. It was the dangerous criminal, public enemy number one. He was the one tugging on my arm. He was up to no good. The snake was attempting to get at my pistol. Instantly my reflexes took over and I jerked my body away from the danger and at the same time I drove my elbow back into the seat to protect my revolver and break his grip on my arm. "What do you think you're doing?" I yelled and leapt to my feet. My sudden spurt of activity caused my Stetson to fall from my head. It landed on the floor between the boy and myself. I stumbled into the aisle as I reached for my pistol. I clawed leather furiously and cursed like a trooper trying to open the flap on the holster to free my weapon. The dangerous criminal recoiled away from me like he had just been hit with a bucket of scalding water. He slammed up against the window and stuck there like putty. For the first time since I had met him, he did not look calm or peaceful. Plastered against the window he looked positively terrified, like suddenly he feared for his life. I knew the feeling, for my heart was pounding a mile a minute.

"I'm sorry, sir," he pleaded apologetically. "I thought you was asleep and I...I just thought you'd like to know that the train is just pulling into Saskatoon. I'm sorry if I startled you."

"Huh," I replied and looked out the window. Sure enough there were buildings all over the place. "Oh yeah. We're in Saskatoon. Right." I reached down and picked up my Stetson and sheepishly returned to my seat.

I quickly looked at our travelling companions. The lady was looking at me like I had suddenly lost my mind. In her eyes, too, I could see fear. Not fear of public enemy number one, but fear of me. For the love of Pete, this woman was afraid of me. I was the cause of her concern. The little boy slept soundly on the seat beside her.

I was wide awake now, and stayed awake for the rest of the trip. I stayed awake on the flight to Prince Albert. In Prince Albert, on my first and last trip to the pen, I turned the dangerous criminal over to the jailer. He looked to be very relieved that he was finally rid of me. On the flight back to Saskatoon I was awake and I was awake on the train ride back to Kindersley. Back in Kindersley, I was awake, but I was ready for bed. Man, I don't know when I had been so happy to see a bed as when I walked back into my room. I couldn't wait to hit the sack.

"Am I ever glad to see you," one of my roommates called out to me as I flopped on the bed. "For a while there, I thought I was going to have to work your shift."

"Enjoy yourself," I replied. "I'm not working any more shifts, I'm going to bed, then I'm packin' up and heading out. Tomorrow morning I'll be in Regina to turn in my kit and sign off. The way I see it, I'd say I've pulled my last shift in the force. From now on it's going to be Bob Adams, private citizen."

"If you want out of this outfit anywhere in the near future, you'd better haul your butt over to the office and report for duty," he chuckled. "You know what they say happens to gold bricks? I know I certainly wouldn't want to be caught sleeping on my last shift."

It was one dozy poor excuse for a human being that pulled his last shift in Kindersley. It had been one very long, trying exercise to keep my eyes open. Finally, the day mercifully drew to an end. It was early evening when I finished my last shift and was saying my goodbys. The last two duties were to thank the corporal and pack my new Volkswagen and beetle off out of there. "Thanks for your help in getting me out of here short and sweet," I said to the corporal as I shook his hand goodby.

"No problem, son," he smiled. "It was my pleasure. I always try to help my men wherever possible. I find that a little cooperation amongst the troops goes a long way."

"I can't argue with you there," I replied. "If you're ever in Alberta, and I can do anything for you, give me a call."

"Well," he smiled, "I sort of figured you'd feel that way, so I took the liberty of volunteering you to drop off a package in Saskatoon tonight."

"What do you mean, volunteered me to go to Saskatoon?" I stammered. "A package? Tonight? You want me to take a package to Saskatoon tonight? But that's not even in the same direction as Regina. I'm sorry, I can't do that. I have to be in Regina in the morning and...."

221

"You can do it, son," he assured me.

"Man, corp, if I go to Saskatoon, I'll never make it to Regina. If I miss my appointment, I'll never get out. They'll have me doing all sorts of dirty duties. I'll probably end up cutting the lawn with a pair of scissors or something like that. Please corp, man, I'll rot before they let me go."

"Come, come now, lad. You're exaggerating. Blowing everything out of proportion," he chuckled. "You run along now and pack your car and stop back here for the package on your way out of town."

"But, I'll have to wear my uniform and I've already got most of it packed."

"Nah," he replied and waved his hand. "Forget the uniform. Wear your civvies."

"Please, corp," I whined. "Can't someone else do it?"

"Hurry along now," he urged. "You don't want to be late for your appointment in Regina. Every minute you dally around here is a minute lost."

I should have asked more questions about the nature of the package before I packed my car. Back at the office, I had to re-pack to make room in the front seat, for this package had two legs and walked out to greet me. One look at my new travelling companion, a prisoner, was enough to tell me that he was certainly different from the previous one. I was not at all keen on having this wild-eyed wiry individual occupying one of the seats in my brand-new Volkswagen Beetle. I noticed that he had trouble written all over him by the way he had to be assisted by the escorting member. "What's the scoop on this guy?" I asked as I watched the escort wrestle with the prisoner to get him into the front seat.

"He's okay. He's harmless," was the strained response. "Don't worry about him. Once you start driving, he'll do exactly what he's told."

"I can see that," I replied somewhat sarcastically. "He looks like a real sweetheart."

The prisoner gave me a little sneer as I crawled in behind the wheel and looked at him. There was no doubt in my mind that he had decided only one of us was going to enjoy this trip and it wasn't going to be me. Suddenly I wished that I had my handgun with me. There was no comfort in knowing that it was securely packed in the trunk in the front of the beetle. This bird was far too cocky for my liking. I decided that I should set the record straight and let him know that only one of us in the Beetle was in control, and it wasn't him. "Well, I certainly hope I make it to Saskatoon this time," I mumbled out loud as I turned the key in the ignition and started to drive away.

"Whaddaya mean, 'you hope you make it this time'?" snickered my passenger.

"Oh nothin'," I replied as I pushed the accelerator to the floor. "It's just that...well, they usually don't let me do escorts. For some reason, I keep losing the prisoners."

"Is that right?" he laughed. "You let a prisoner escape or something?"

"Not exactly," I replied. The tires squealed as I skidded the Beetle onto the highway. My passenger clawed the air for something to hold onto in an attempt to remain in his seat. "I have this bad habit, I keep falling asleep. That's why I have to use my own car now. It's cheaper for them to pay me mileage than to replace a patrol car." I put a little more pressure on the accelerator and swerved across the road and onto the shoulder. "Whoa," I yelled and slapped myself on the side of the face. Then I grabbed the steering wheel in both hands and whipped it around, first one way, then the other before I steadied the little Beetle and we raced toward Saskatoon."Whoo wee! Now that was close," I whistled and shook my head as if to clear the cob-webs.

"Are you crazy or something?" asked my passenger. His eyes were glued to the road and his face was white as snow.

As we passed a side road, I noticed that someone had been in the ditch and chewed up the ground pretty good. "See that," I said and leaned back over the seat. I was looking out the back window and trying to point to the spot we had just passed. "That's where I hit the ditch the last trip." In my attempt to show him the sight, the Beetle had sort of drifted across the highway and was just about to enter the far ditch.

"Look out," yelled my package.

I turned back to the road and just in the nick of time I was able to pull back onto the highway. The cockiness was gone. He didn't look like he would be much trouble for the rest of the trip.

"You just sit back and relax," I replied as I calmly reached into the back seat to adjust some of my belongings that had shifted during my earlier manoeuvres. He'll be alright now, I chuckled as the telephone poles flicked by like a picket fence and the poor soul was white-knuckling it. One hand was clamped on the door handle, the other on the dash. "I suppose it's got to be comforting to know that you're in good hands when you take a trip like this," I casually mentioned. "But you should talk to me. It helps keep me awake."

There was no fear of falling asleep after that little revelation. My travelling companion suddenly developed verbal diarrhea. He talked, he sang and he told jokes. His jaw flapped nonstop as his eyes flashed between me and the road. By the time we reached Saskatoon, I knew more than enough about that boy.

It was after midnight when I dropped my package off and left Saskatoon heading for Regina. It was a beautiful fall night. The skies were clear and the moon and stars shone bright as I drove along Highway 11 between Saskatoon and Regina.

About halfway between Saskatoon and Regina the lights of Davidson, Saskatchewan appeared on the horizon. It meant nothing really, for I had learned a long time ago that to see the lights of a town in Saskatchewan did not mean that the town was close. To the contrary, on that flat prairie landscape, it was probably a hundred miles away.

I passed the time singing along with some country singers on the radio and dreaming about my new career. In fact, I believe I was dreaming about doing some real field work. I was on my way to Brooks, on the Alberta prairie. It was the fall of the year and I was imagining myself driving out across the countryside checking animals and hunters. I could even feel myself bouncing across the grasslands chasing after a herd of Pronghorn Antelope. The prairie looked flat and smooth, but looks can be deceiving. In my dreams I was being tossed around pretty good.

Then I realized it was not a dream. This was for real. I was driving on a very rough surface, being tossed around in my brand-new Volkswagen Beetle. In fact, the Beetle was acting like a bucking bronco. Suddenly the steering wheel spun in my hands and jammed one thumb. That was the final wake-up call as I bounced about like a rubber ball being tossed around on the inside of the car. I clutched the steering wheel, hanging on for dear life as I slammed on the brakes. There was no screeching of tires as the little Beetle bounced and finally shuddered to a stop. I looked around to see what had happened as a cloud of dust engulfed my brand-new Volkswagen Beetle. I was parked a long way from the highway, out in the middle of some farmer's summer fallow field. The lights of Davidson, Saskatchewan were no longer in the distance. They were right in front of me.

In the wee hours of the morning, in the middle of a field in Saskatchewan, I was wide awake.

I chose not to think of what might have been on that September night. Instead, I stared into the lights of Davidson and saw the brightness of the future, my future as a Fish Cop.

ROBERT J. (BOB) ADAMS

Bob Adams was born in Turner Valley, Alberta in 1938. He grew up in the Edson area, in a log house, built by his father on a farm rich in swamp spruce, tamarack, willows and muskeg.

Bob, an avid outdoorsman, was one of the fortunate few who was able to live his boyhood dreams as he entered the workforce. In 1960, after a number of years with the Alberta Forest Service and Royal Canadian Mounted Police, he began a career with Provincial Government as a Fish and Wildlife Office. For the next 33 years, he found his homes to include Brooks, Strathmore, Hinton, Calgary, Peace River and Edmonton.

In 1993, after a full career in Enforcement, he retired from Fish and Wildlife and wrote his first book, The Stump Farm. Today, Bob resides in Edmonton, Alberta with his wife Martha where he continues to work on his writing.

GIVE A **"ROBERT J. ADAMS"** BOOK TO A FRIEND

Megamy Publishing Ltd.
Box 3507
Spruce Grove, AB   T7X 3A7

Send to:
Name:_____

Street:_____

City:_____
Province/   Postal/
State:_____ Zip Code:_____

Please send:
"The Stump Farm"   ____ @ $14.95 = _____

"Beyond the Stump Farm" ____ @ $14.95 = _____

"Horse Cop"   ____ @ $15.95 = _____
Shipping and handling per book @ $ 4.00 = _____
                                7% GST   = _____
                Total amount enclosed: _____

Make cheque or money order payable to:
Megamy Publishing Ltd.
Price subject to change without prior notice.
ORDERS OUTSIDE OF CANADA must be paid in U.S. funds by
cheque or money order drawn on U.S. or Canadian Bank.
Sorry no C.O.D.'s.

Gift from:
Name:_____

Address:_____

City:_____
Province/   Postal/
State:_____ Zip Code:_____

Megamy Publishing will gladly enclose your personal
message with each book sent as a gift.

GIVE A **"ROBERT J. ADAMS"** BOOK TO A FRIEND

Megamy Publishing Ltd.
Box 3507
Spruce Grove, AB   T7X 3A7

Send to:
Name:_____

Street:_____

City:_____
Province/   Postal/
State:_____ Zip Code:_____

Please send:
  "The Stump Farm"   ____ @ $14.95 = _____

  "Beyond the Stump Farm" ____ @ $14.95 = _____

  "Horse Cop"   ____ @ $15.95 = _____
Shipping and handling per book @ $ 4.00 = _____
                           7% GST   = _____
              Total amount enclosed: _____

Make cheque or money order payable to:
Megamy Publishing Ltd.
Price subject to change without prior notice.
ORDERS OUTSIDE OF CANADA must be paid in U.S. funds by
cheque or money order drawn on U.S. or Canadian Bank.
Sorry no C.O.D.'s.

Gift from:
Name:_____

Address:_____

City:_____
Province/   Postal/
State:_____ Zip Code:_____

Megamy Publishing will gladly enclose your personal
message with each book sent as a gift.

GIVE A **"ROBERT J. ADAMS"** BOOK TO A FRIEND

Megamy Publishing Ltd.
Box 3507
Spruce Grove, AB   T7X 3A7

Send to:
Name: _____

Street: _____

City: _____

Province/   Postal/
State: _____ Zip Code: _____

Please send:
   "The Stump Farm"   _____ @ $14.95 = _____

   "Beyond the Stump Farm" _____ @ $14.95 = _____

   "Horse Cop"   _____ @ $15.95 = _____
Shipping and handling per book @ $ 4.00 = _____
                           7% GST   = _____
                Total amount enclosed: _____

Make cheque or money order payable to:
Megamy Publishing Ltd.
Price subject to change without prior notice.
ORDERS OUTSIDE OF CANADA must be paid in U.S. funds by
cheque or money order drawn on U.S. or Canadian Bank.
Sorry no C.O.D.'s.

Gift from:
Name: _____

Address: _____

City: _____
Province/   Postal/
State: _____ Zip Code: _____

Megamy Publishing will gladly enclose your personal
message with each book sent as a gift.

GIVE A "ROBERT J. ADAMS" BOOK TO A FRIEND

Megamy Publishing Ltd.
Box 3507
Spruce Grove, AB   T7X 3A7

Send to:
Name:_____

Street:_____

City:_____
Province/   Postal/
State:_____ Zip Code:_____

Please send:

  "The Stump Farm"   ____@ $14.95 = _____

  "Beyond the Stump Farm" ____@ $14.95 = _____

  "Horse Cop"   ____@ $15.95 = _____
Shipping and handling per book @ $ 4.00 = _____
                    7% GST   = _____
           Total amount enclosed: _____

Make cheque or money order payable to:
Megamy Publishing Ltd.
Price subject to change without prior notice.
ORDERS OUTSIDE OF CANADA must be paid in U.S. funds by
cheque or money order drawn on U.S. or Canadian Bank.
Sorry no C.O.D.'s.

Gift from:
Name:_____

Address:_____

City:_____
Province/   Postal/
State:_____Zip Code:_____

Megamy Publishing will gladly enclose your personal
message with each book sent as a gift.

GIVE A **"ROBERT J. ADAMS"** BOOK TO A FRIEND

Megamy Publishing Ltd.
Box 3507
Spruce Grove, AB   T7X 3A7

Send to:
Name:_____

Street:_____

City:_____
Province/   Postal/
State:_____ Zip Code:_____

Please send:
  "The Stump Farm" _____ @ $14.95 = _____

  "Beyond the Stump Farm" _____ @ $14.95 = _____

  "Horse Cop" _____ @ $15.95 = _____
  Shipping and handling per book @ $ 4.00 = _____
                          7% GST   = _____
              Total amount enclosed: _____

Make cheque or money order payable to:
Megamy Publishing Ltd.
Price subject to change without prior notice.
ORDERS OUTSIDE OF CANADA must be paid in U.S. funds by
cheque or money order drawn on U.S. or Canadian Bank.
Sorry no C.O.D.'s.

Gift from:
Name:_____

Address:_____

City:_____
Province/   Postal/
State:_____Zip Code:_____

Megamy Publishing will gladly enclose your personal
message with each book sent as a gift.